THE RUG HOOK BOOK

A Sterling/Lark Book

First paperback edition published in 1994 by
Sterling Publishing Company, Inc.
387 Park Avenue South, New York, N.Y. 10016

Produced and © 1992 by Altamont Press, Inc.
50 College Street, Asheville, N.C.

Editing: Thom Boswell
Design: Chris Colando, Thom Boswell
Production: Chris Colando
Illustrations: Chris Colando
Photography: Evan Bracken

Every effort has been made to ensure that all the
information in this book is accurate. However, due
to differing conditions, tools, and individual skills,
the publisher cannot be responsible for any injuries,
losses, and other damages which may result from
the use of the information in this book.

Library of Congress CIP Data Available

10 9 8 7 6

Distributed in Canada by Sterling Publishing
% Canadian Manda Group
P.O. Box 920, Station U
Toronto, Ontario, Canada M8Z 5P9
Distributed in Great Britain and Europe by
Cassell PLC, Villiers House, 41/47 Strand
London WC2N 5JE, England
Distributed in Australia by Capricorn Link
(Australia) Pty Ltd., P.O. Box 6651
Baulkham Hills, Business Centre
NSW 2153, Australia

Sterling ISBN 0-8069-8358-2 Trade
0-8069-8359-0 Paper

Pineapple Antique (36"x72") Primitive rug hooked and designed by Marion Ham.

THE RUG HOOK BOOK

TECHNIQUES, PROJECTS AND PATTERNS FOR THIS EASY, TRADITIONAL CRAFT

A Sterling/Lark Book
Sterling Publishing Co., Inc.   New York

Edited by
Thom Boswell

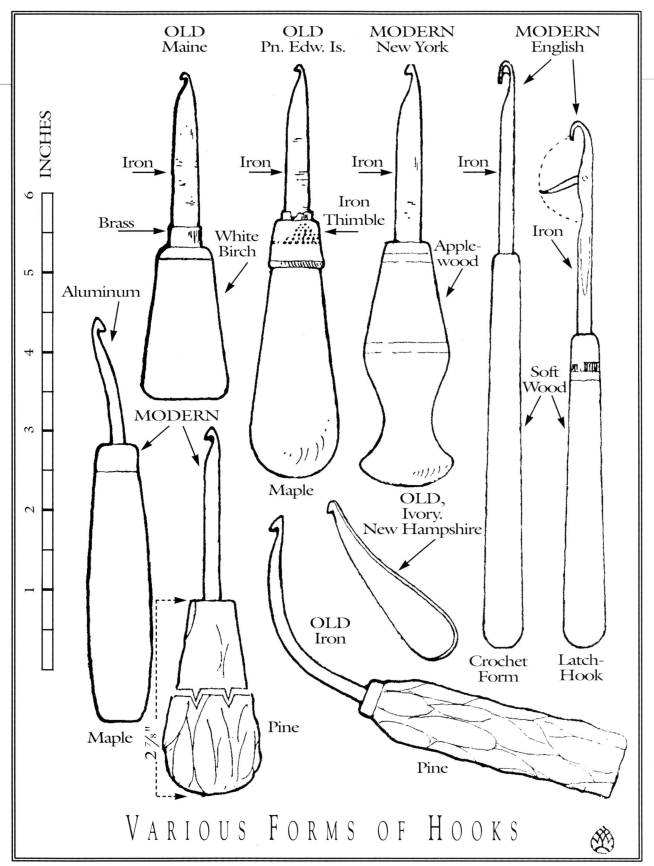

INCHES
6 5 4 3 2 1

OLD
Maine

OLD
Pn. Edw. Is.

MODERN
New York

MODERN
English

Iron

Iron

Iron

Iron

Iron

Iron
Thimble

Brass

White
Birch

Aluminum

Apple-
wood

Soft
Wood

MODERN

Maple

Maple

OLD,
Ivory.
New Hampshire

OLD
Iron

Crochet
Form

Latch-
Hook

Maple

2 7⁄8"

Pine

Pine

VARIOUS FORMS OF HOOKS

Illustration of old hooks from W.W. Kent's book, *The Hooked Rug.*

TABLE OF CONTENTS

Rug hooking has been around a few hundred years—probably longer—but it is catching on again with a new fervor. This may be because it is a craft that is so easy to pick up, yet the opportunities for advancing one's technique and expressing one's creativity are so enticing. And of course, the rugs *are* usable—on floors and even as wall hangings.

The investment in tools and materials is quite small, although you may elect to upgrade them as you proceed. Actually, there's a good chance that after thumbing through this book, you could scare up a few items around the

The Things I Love **(21" x 28"), primitive hooking and design by Tanya Azzaro, 13 years old. (Above)**

Amelia **(24" x 34"), traditional hooking by Lorna Smith, designed by Jane McGown Flynn. (Left)**

house and start practicing today.

The craft of rug hooking is also uniquely accessible because there are so many ways you can approach it. You can draw your own design or draw on countless other sources. You can use fabric scraps from worn out clothing, dye your own colors, or buy fine woolens that are pre-cut and dyed to your specifications. You can buy kits that come complete with materials and instructions , or you can transcend both primitive and traditional techniques and experiment on the cutting edge of contemporary design with alternative materials and construction.

For some, rug hooking may be a relaxing escape from the day's worries. Rug hooking qualifies nicely as a "pick-up" craft.

That is, you don't need large blocks of scheduled time to hook. It is very easy to stop and start again when you have the time to continue, because there is no counting or figuring needed to tell you where you must pick it up. Nonetheless, all rug hookers are free to seek their own level of involvement.

You may find the opportunity to learn rug hooking first hand from a teacher in your area. Rug hooking retreats are also available for those wishing some intensive study of rug hooking. However, for today's busy person trying to juggle a career and family, it is still possible to learn the craft without spending hours in classes learning techniques for hooking, dyeing and designing. One must not be intimidated by what appears to be a long list of prerequisites. Simply by reading this book and learning by doing, you can quickly join the ranks of homegrown hookers who, like our ancestors whose rugs we find so charming, add to a rich heritage of artistic expression.

Within these pages you will find all the basic information you need to hook rugs, a couple of dozen illustrated projects with ample instructions, a wealth of raw patterns to interpret, a gallery of rug hooking artist's work to inspire, and other resources to support your own creative efforts. May you hook long and well, and most happily.

Queen Mary (4'x6') hooked by B.J. Andreas, designed by Pearl McGown.

Khursan (26"x25') runner, hooked by B.J. Andreas, designed by Jane Flynn.

The history of rug hooking is not without controversy. Most authorities appear to agree, however, that the craft was utilitarian in origin. W. W. Kent, an early 20th century author and authority on hooked rugs, traced the roots of rug hooking through an example of a 6th century Coptic mat, implying a lineage to ancient Egypt. Evidence of the craft cropped up in medieval Spain through northern Africa, and is documented to have existed in Scotland, northern England and Scandinavia at least four centuries ago. Hooking became quite popular in early 19th century England in the form of hearth rugs. To quote Kent: "Many dwellings, especially cottages where no other rug or carpet was used had the hearth rug. Of all men, the Englishman, whatever his lot in life, has always loved his fireside and valued all that embellished it, or added to its comfortable aspect. Hence, among rugs, the hearth rug, from pelt to textile, has in England long held an important place."

Opponents of this theory contend that rug hooking is indigenous to colonial North America. Before burlap became commonly available in the mid-1800s, feed sacks provided the foundations for most early hooked rugs, into which the scraps of worn out clothing were hooked. Coastal New Englanders and Canadians of the maritime provinces found great appeal in this new craft. Seafaring men, as well as their wives and sweethearts left ashore, were eager to try their hand at hooking during their long months at sea, using foundations of canvas and strands of yarn or rope. (One might wonder if some poor dismembered sea captain might have found solace in this craft with an aptly fitted appendage.)

The people who drew their own hooking patterns were not overly concerned with their artistic ability, or lack thereof. Consequently, most of the early patterns had a whimsical flair. There was very little concern for perspective—a dog could be towering over the house by which it stood, or a bird could be bigger than a tree. The larger object was usually placed in a prominent location, usually near the center of the rug, thus suggesting its importance.

The subjects used to inspire designs for hooked rugs were as varied as the people who hooked them. Often, familiar objects were chosen as subjects: homes, favorite pets, a scenic garden or even family members. Anniversaries and other special occasions were sometimes commemorated in a rug. Not all of the themes, however, were based on happy memories. In fact, some rugs show a degree of bitterness and appear to be a creative outlet for the artist's displeasure with some aspect of her life. The intent of the designer is clear, at times, as words or poems are hooked right into the design. Although we cannot always interpret the original intent of the artist, we can be sure the rugs provide us with insight into her life at the time they were hooked.

Life in the 1850s was a challenge even to the most competent individual. Hooked rugs kept the floor warm and kept drafts out. The fact that they added a decorative touch to an otherwise drab environment was an added pleasure. Although the utility of a hooked rug is no longer considered to be a motivating force for the novice crafter, the emotional satisfaction of rug hooking continues to remain high. So it was that an enterprising peddler from Maine, Edward Sands Frost, noticed the housewives of this period hooking functional rugs with enthusiasm, but often without adequate tools or designs. After machining a superior hook for his own wife, he hit on the notion of mass producing design stencils out of tin which he sold from his wagon along his sales route. Although these standard patterns displaced some of the need for creativity, the practice of rug hooking flourished more extensively as a result. Another New Englander, Ralph Burnham, furthered the

Currier & Ives' Winter Road (25" x 38"), from a Yankee Peddler design, Yankee Peddler Collection.

The Vessel (24" x 28"), hooked by Frieda Powers from a Yankee Peddler design, Yankee Peddler Collection.

craft by repairing thousands of old hooked rugs and selling more patterns in the early 20th century.

The old primitive style of hooking with wider strips and simpler patterns remains the most popular technique practiced today. The traditional style (also known as fine, artistic, realistic, and shaded hooking) has evolved as a more challenging version of hooking, involving the use of narrower strips, more sophisticated designs, and intricate use of color and shading. A third approach, usually referred to as contemporary, encourages open experimentation with all aspects of what we have come to regard as rug hooking. All rug hooking continues to be an artistic commentary on our changing lifestyles and culture.

1840 House (24" x 36"), rug hooked and designed by Jacqueline Hansen, 1991.

JACQUELINE LEMIEUX HANSEN

Rug hooking began as a hobby, and was added to my already established business of Interior Decorating at the "Georgian House" located in Westbrook, Maine. I had extensive art training in pastels, ink drawing, watercolor, and oil painting, and studied rug hooking with Pearl McGown of Worcester, MA.

Later I moved to Scarborough, where my shop is now known as "The 1840 House." I teach rug hooking classes at all levels and offer special workshops throughout the year, locally and around the country. Requests for special designs led me to publish a design catalog, "Jacqueline Designs—for the Joy of Hooking," containing over 350 designs. Custom coloring of wool and designing are part of my catalog business. My video, "How to Hook," has been popular with people without the benefit of teachers in their area.

Bird and House (26" x 40"), primitive rug hooked and designed by Jacqueline Hansen, 1987.

10

Sea Urchins (26" x 39),
traditional rug hooked and
designed by Jacqueline Hansen,
1990.

Waldoboro Floral (24" x 36")
features a family pet, hooked
and designed by Jacqueline
Hansen, 1989.

NANCY MILLER

I love my life as a rug hooker, instructor, and supplier. At times I am surprised at having this career, as my perspective of rug hooking has changed dramatically through the years. As a young child, I viewed my grandmother as having a very boring life, sitting hour after hour bent over her frame. I delighted in attending the state fair each year and seeing her blue ribbon rugs, but had no thought of ever taking up the craft. When my mother started hooking I still did not take much notice. But now I am a full-time teacher and supplier, and my home is decorated with beautiful rugs of my own, my mother, grandmother, and great-grandmother.

I began hooking out of boredom while recovering from an accident, and was surprised by the tranquil therapy and artistic expression it provided. I quickly became "hooked." I developed an appreciation for the art and discovered the satisfaction of creating heirlooms. A year after returning to my job, I resigned to attempt a career in rug hooking.

Wildflowers **(24" x 36"), traditional rug hooked by Nancy Miller, designed by Jane Flynn, instructed by Maryanne Lincoln.**

My preference in design has been for florals. I am surprised at how easily they can be developed with proper instruction and properly dyed woolens. I owe much of my ability to the McGown National Guild, as my training has come from attending their workshops and rug schools.

Genevive **(14" x 24" unfinished), traditional hooking by Nancy Miller, designed by Jane Flynn, instructed by Betty Maley.**

ANN WINTERLING

The wallhangings and rugs I hook are my own designs and are inspired by personal history. Never undertaken to fill a specific space or need, I think of my work as textile art where enjoyment comes from the challenge of solving problems in creating the piece. Memories of my family and favorite places are kept alive for me by hooking them into a design.

In *Grandfather's Farm*, memories of the scene (the house and barn, cows, orchard, the mountains, and grandfather picking blueberries), are transformed and connected to the way I view things today by creating a brightly colored piece with a folk art quality and a vigorous textural hooking technique. This is the latest work in my twenty years of hooking.

To make my work visually entertaining, I use a variety of shapes, juxtaposition of lightest and darkest values, high impact color, enough detail to keep the viewer interested as well as some expanses to rest the eye.

I use a simple hook and cut 100% wool which is hand-dyed and hooked by pulling one loop at a time through the backing. For backings I use 100% cotton monk's cloth or linen for durability.

Grandfather's Farm (29" x 37"), **textural hooking and design by Ann Winterling, 1991.**

13

MARION N. HAM

After about 25 years of hooking rugs, what I'm known for is the original art form of making rugs in America. The distinction with early American rug hooking is the strips cut from old fabric, the naivete of the pattern and the use of many textures. I think it truly is an art form because it's very creative and it's very expressive and colorful.

It's a craft that's personalized. It is group therapy for people to get together like they did in years gone by at quilting bees. It's producing an item that becomes an heirloom. It provides the accent in a home. And it's very attractive with colonial type furnishings. Or you can hook a contemporary style or make it very ornate to go with Victorian furniture and style. It fits into almost any category.

Cherries and Sheep (29-1/2" x 52"), **primitive rug hooked and designed by Marion Ham.**

Homestead (34" x 70"), **primitive rug hooked and designed by Marion Ham.**

Sudbury (36" x 56"), primitive rug hooked by Marion Ham. (*Above*)

Pomegranate, primitive rug hooked and designed by Marion Ham. (*Left*)

Tree of Birds (... x 50"), traditi... tapestry hook... by Meredith LeBeau, Yank... Peddler Studi...

16

Meredith Pauling LeBeau

For me, traditional rug hooking is an essential part of life. I have always felt the need to create, and after many attempts at a variety of handcrafts, I found this to be my method of expression. To take flat pieces of wool and turn them into realistic flowers, fruit, animals or pastoral scenes is truly exciting to me. It doesn't matter what the subject, the challenge is the same. Most of my work involves fine shading, and that is what I enjoy the most. I have studied and taught this type of hooking for many years, and have been greatly influenced by my teacher, Ethel Bruce of Haverhill, MA. It is she who taught me the subtle use of color which I feel elevates our craft to an art.

My hooked pieces are my unwritten diary. I can instantly recall exactly what was happening in my life while any particular piece was being developed. *The Yankee Peddler*, pictured here, was hooked mostly after midnight. It was the only time that was left over from very busy family days. I have a leaf on a crewel design wall hanging that resembles an enormous grin. I was watching the inauguration of Jimmy Carter the day that I hooked it. And, so it goes.

There will never be enough time to actually execute all of my ideas. But I find that simply exploring with my mind brings pleasure. I look forward to many more years of development; but some days, just to dream is sufficient.

The Yankee Peddler (38" x 64-1/2"), **traditional wall hanging hooked by Meredith LeBeau, Yankee Peddler Studio.**

JANE OLSON

I have been hooking traditional rugs since the 1930s. My teaching activity spans 35 years, having received my teaching credentials from UCLA and taught in the California School Department for 15 years. I've held classes in my rug hooking shop ever since my retirement.

I design rugs, dye commercial swatches, and have published several books pertaining to rug hooking, braiding and dyeing. This includes my bi-monthly Rugger's Roundtable instruction newsletter which features my patterns. I have lectured at meetings of the Association of Traditional Hooking Artists, Guild meetings and Weaving Guilds, and have instructed at workshops all over the United States and Canada for more than 15 years.

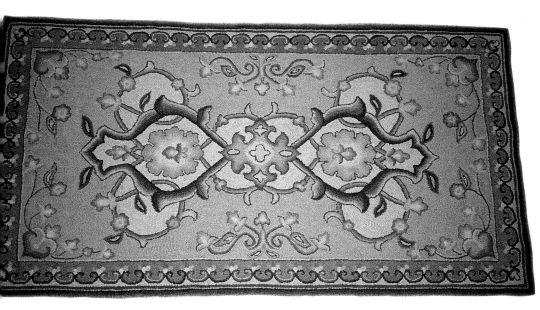

Persian Paisley (60" x 84"), traditional rug hooked and designed by Jane Olson. (*Opposite*)

Memories (24" x 30"), traditional wall piece hooked by Jane Olson from a Paul Detlefsen print. (*Above*)

Parthian (36" x 60"), traditional rug hooked by Jane Olson from a Persian design. (*Left*)

19

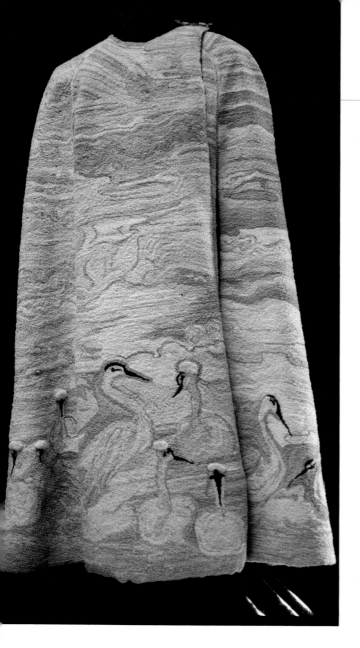

a memory of Sadako and the legend of 1,000 paper cranes, full length cape, fine hooking and design by M.S. Burton. (*Above, Left*)

Kountry Korner Kappers (10' x 12'), primitive with fine details hooked and designed by M.S. Burton, from Shaker children's alphabet. (*Above, Right*)

Angel sculpture, traditional hooking by M.S. Burton. (*Below, Right*)

MARY SHEPPARD BURTON

Sadako Sasaki's life was so short. Tender, loving, and full of vitality, she laboriously folded paper cranes with the hope of overcoming the dreadful atomic disease, leukemia. Sadako never completed her dream of hope—to fold a thousand paper cranes and to be whole again. At the age of twelve she slipped into another world. Her classmates sent with her an additional three hundred and fifty-six cranes so that the full count of a thousand might aid her entry into eternity.

A monument in Sadako's honor stands in Hiroshima Peace Park where on August 6th, thousands of paper cranes encircle the monument to remember the child who so loved life. As I watched the cranes fly above the shores of Japan I understood the legend of Sadako and the thousand paper cranes. Their massive eight and nine foot wing span was awesome. It brought to the mind and heart the power of the will to live, the memory of the legend, the wishes of a child and the hope of all of us for the tomorrows. Thus this mantle dreamed by the right side of my mind has become the symbol of my own inner will to live fully.

Detail from *Alpha, Beta, Omega* (28" x 13'), traditional runner hooked by M.S. Burton, design adapted from 18th century American alphabet. (*Above*)

***Moghul Taj*, traditional hooking by M.S. Burton, adapted from a Persian design. (*Left*)**

SALLY ANN CORBETT

I began hooking rugs in 1980 with purchased swatches and patterns. In 1986 I realized that the only rugs I finished were ones that I designed myself. Since then I have been doing almost exclusively my own designs. I am drawn to pictorial pieces that tell a story, so my rugs end up hanging on my walls rather than on the floor.

Probably the single thing that has influenced my style most was a large amount of cut wool, given to me by a woman who was no longer hooking. I stored it for six years, moved it to three different homes, and finally decided I needed to get rid of it once and for all. I decided to use it in a geometric "fish scale" design. Since I had bags and bags of seemingly unrelated strips of wool, I had to figure out how to put them together without them looking garish. Now my preference is to cut up all different weights, textures and colors of wool, put them in boxes sorted by color, and then hook them together into a picture. I will overdye my wool, but rarely will I hook from a straight gradated color swatch anymore.

Experimenting with color is my favorite part of rug hooking, and the more I work with color, the more I feel that there are no "ugly" colors. I just have to find that perfect combination to make it sing!

Before the Ball (35" x 47"), mixed-cut shaded hooking and design by Sally Corbett, 1992; photo by Gary Quinn. (*Left*)

Sunset on the Sequim Prairie (35" x 47"), primitive shaded hooking and design by Sally Corbett, 1991; photo by Gary Quinn (*Opposite*).

Fishing on the Silver Colorado (31" x 40"), primitive shaded hooking and design by Sally Corbett, 1991; photo by Gary Quinn (*Right*)

CHRIS MERRYMAN

Many people think of winter in the north as being bleak and barren. I designed and hooked *Puget Sound—Winter* to remind us of how much life *is* present, and that we should work to save such beauty and abundance. Nineteen indigenous winter shorebirds are shown approximately 2/3 their actual size.

The rug is made totally of recycled wool fabric. This is a goal I use as much as possible in all my work. All the birds were made with "as-is" wool fabric, except the cormorant which was overdyed. In addition to many solid colors, I have used more than 40 checks, tweeds, and plaids to hook the birds. The background consists of 170 square feet of recycled skirts, shirts, blankets, jackets, etc., all over-dyed with the same dye.

As were the original hooked rugs, it represents what is special to me. It was made for, and is used on, the floor.

The Cranes of Kingsway (28" x 41"), primitive shaded rug, hooked and designed by Chris Merryman, 1991; photo by Tom Merryman. (*Above*)

Sonora Spring (26" x 38"), primitive shaded rug, hooked and designed by Chris Merryman, 1991; photo by Tom Merryman. (*Left*)

Puget Sound—Winter
(6' oval), primitive shaded
rug, hooked and designed by
Chris Merryman, 1991;
photo by Tom Merryman.

ROSLYN LOGSDON

I think of my hooked wall hangings as paintings because I started out as a painter many years ago. Rug hooking adds a tactile quality to the two-dimensional surface that cannot be achieved with paint.

The images I work with (people and architectural elements) take me in two different directions, though sometimes I combine both. In any case, I am always concerned with the relationships between each of these elements. On another level, and the reason these images are hooked rather than painted, is the relationship between the different fabrics used to create the surface—solids, heathers, tweeds, plaids, etc.

The surfaces achieved in rughooking are unique to fiber techniques. Something special happens when a plaid or herringbone is cut into strips and hooked into loops that create surfaces and shadows. I like working in a close color or tonal range so that I have to find diversity within the textural surfaces. My images captured in wool are enhanced by the endlessly varied surfaces achieved by hooking.

Building with Balconies (15-1/2" x 28-1/2"), wall hanging, hooked and designed by Roslyn Logsdon, 1991; photo by Linda Zandler.

Summer Sunday (16-1/2" x 19"), wall hanging, hooked and designed by Roslyn Logsdon, 1991; photo by Linda Zandler. (*Above, Left*)

Home Team (26" x 33"), wall hanging, hooked and designed by Roslyn Logsdon, 1991; photo by Linda Zandler. (*Below, Left*)

Two Women with Dog (20" x 23-1/2"), wall hanging, hooked and designed by Roslyn Logsdon, 1991; photo by Linda Zandler. (*Above, Right*)

PEG IRISH

Rug hooking has become a wonderful way for me to express myself. I love color, texture, and abstract graphic design, which seems especially suited to this medium. I began rug hooking to make some rugs for the floors of my old house, but soon started making wall hangings when I discovered I had a talent for hooking (brought out by several excellent teachers), and could use it to create colorful paintings with wool.

When I began designing my own rugs, I started with simple objects in my life (my cats, dog, and house). Now, most of my designs have a geometric quality. They are simple to draw and provide the greatest freedom to create unusual color plans. My work has become unique because of the control I have over my color planning through a dye system that I developed which allows me to match values of whatever hues I am dyeing. I especially enjoy dyeing and devising interesting color plans for my rug hooking. I also like to use a wide range of textures including wool fabrics, yarns, and special materials such as ribbon and metallic threads to add interest to my work.

Maple Leaf Rag (14-3/4" x 20-3/4"), wool strips and yarn, hooked and designed by Peg Irish, 1990; photo by Andrew Edgar. (*Above*)

Emerging Crocus (18-1/2" x 19-1/4"), mixed media hooked and designed by Peg Irish, 1991; photo by James Irish. (*Right*)

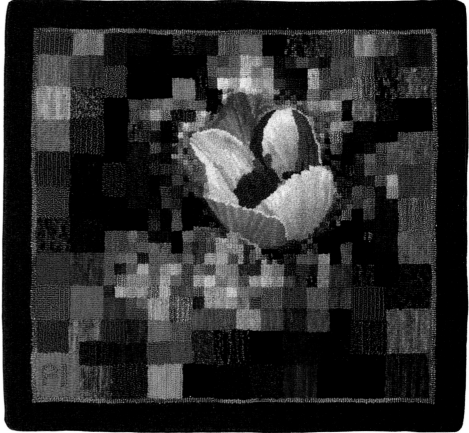

Cat Walk (26" x 27"), traditional hooking and design by Peg Irish, 1990; photo by Andrew Edgar.

GLORIA CROUSE

I'm mad about texture...and art-rugs are my outlet for this love of fiber and a mix of materials! By playing the highs vs. the lows, the smooth vs. the rough, or shiny against dull, the texture of each enhances the other. Along with yarns and yardage, I like to throw in surprise elements—often some metal (construction hardware: washers, wire, rivets, grommets), sometimes a painted ground, or additions of interesting found objects. The demands of a well constructed rug for the floor disciplines the uses of these materials—a basic consideration, always.

In recent work, I've enjoyed breaking away from the typical rectangle and circular forms. Irregular and asymmetric shapes have been delightful to design—plus they allow for many diversified configurations and furniture arrangements. With each turn, a new concept. And why not cut off a corner, if it would be constantly walked upon. From the irregular, I've made several 2-part rugs. These further add to the alternate possibilities of designing shapes and sizes. With such wild variety, no wonder this work never becomes a bore!

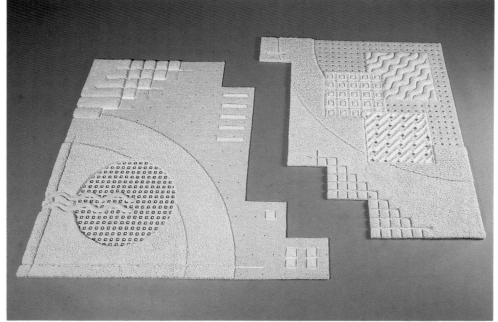

Wild Queendom (36" x 100"), mixed wools, hooked and designed by Gloria Crouse, 1991; photo by Roger Schreiber. (*Above*)

Creme-de-la-Creme (56" x 79", mixed media, adjustable sections, hooked and designed by Gloria Crouse, 1984; photo by Chris Eden. (Collection: Dr. and Mrs. Richard Harding) (*Left*)

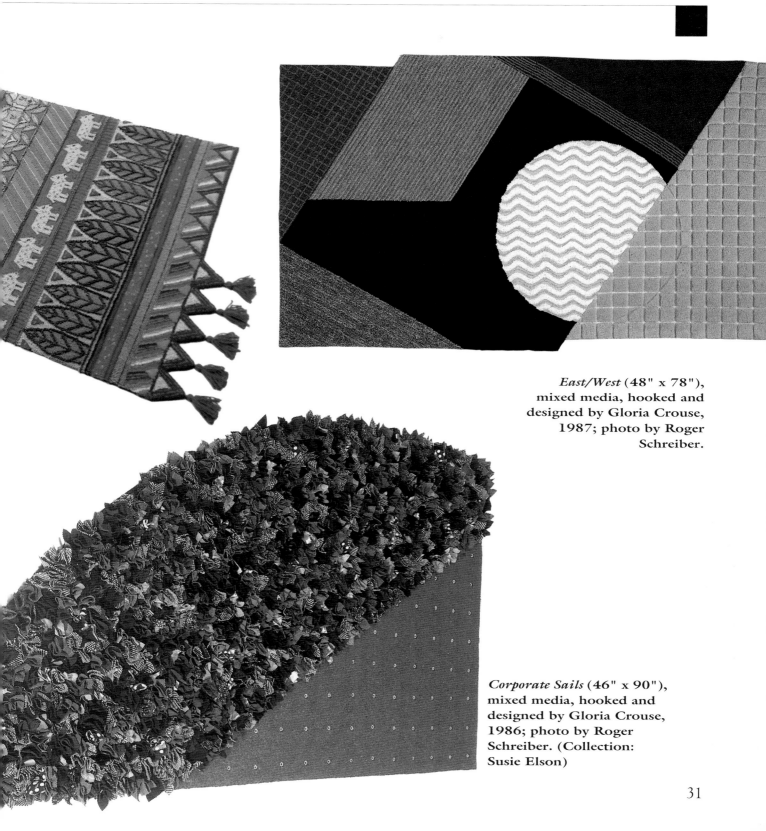

East/West (48" x 78"),
mixed media, hooked and
designed by Gloria Crouse,
1987; photo by Roger
Schreiber.

Corporate Sails (46" x 90"),
mixed media, hooked and
designed by Gloria Crouse,
1986; photo by Roger
Schreiber. (Collection:
Susie Elson)

31

Most of the basic information and primitive techniques were furnished by Beth Sekerka. Some additional information on traditional techniques was contributed by Marie Azzaro, contemporary techniques by Gloria E. Crouse, traditional dyeing information by Maryanne Lincoln, binding and finishing techniques by Anne Ashworth and Jean Armstrong.

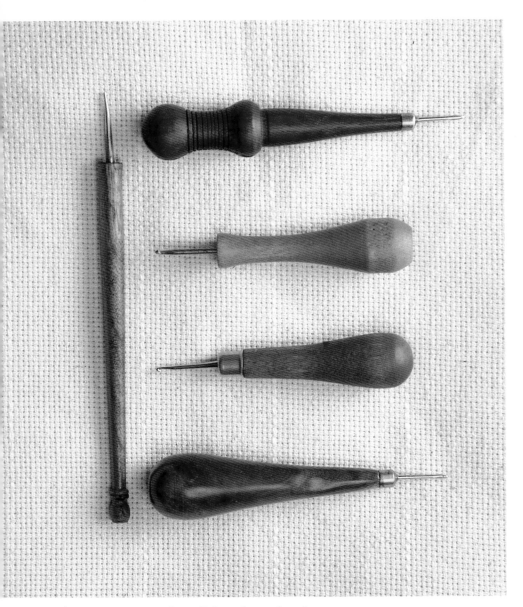

An assortment of traditional rug hooks, courtesy of Nancy Greenberg.

HOOKS

The primary tool you will need is a rug hook. In lieu of a rug hook, you may substitute a metal crochet hook (size F, G, or H). Since it is awkward to use the crochet hook without a handle, you can make a handle by inserting the end of the hook into a pre-drilled wooden handle or dowel. The hook end should extend about one to two inches from the handle, so the other end must be cut off accordingly.

Rug hooks that can be ordered from rug hooking suppliers vary in both the size of the actual hook and the handle. Some hooks have a long pencil-like handle while others have a shorter, rounded handle. This is a matter of personal preference as to which handle is easier to use. The hook varies in size from very fine to rather large. In general, the fine hooks lend themselves better to traditional rug hooking (with yarns and very thin strips of wool) while the larger hooks are better for primitive rug hooking, although a finer hook can also be used. Once again, this will depend on which feels better to you.

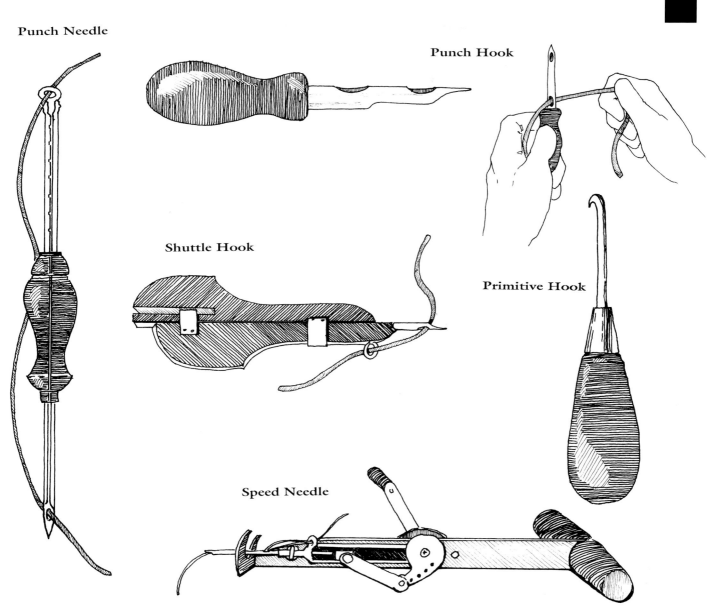

Punch Needle

Punch Hook

Shuttle Hook

Primitive Hook

Speed Needle

There is also a whole family of "speed hooks" which you may find desirable, especially for very large pieces or the more experimental contemporary hooking techniques. Simple punch hooks and punch needles poke yarn or strips through a foundation deep enough so that loops remain when they are withdrawn. The shuttle hook is an ingenious, efficient device that has been around a long time. Threaded with either heavier strips or yarns, it is worked with both hands. There is also a speed needle that has a hand crank like an eggbeater. It can make loops from 1/8 to 7/8 inches long, and accepts fine to medium weight yarns, strips, and even unconventional materials like wire, thread, plastic and paper.

33

FRAMES

You will need a frame to keep your work taut. Any backing that loosens easily in a frame makes hooking more difficult. There are several options in frame design, most of which you can make yourself.

An old pine picture frame provides an easy start for lap work. Place your pattern over the frame and thumb tack the edges. The softness of the pine easily accommodates the tacks. You can also nail your own together with four sticks, or purchase a ready-made canvas-stretcher at an art supply shop.

Quilt enthusiasts probably have access to a 14" quilting hoop. An embroidery hoop is too thin and will not be adequate for rug hooking. While even larger rugs can be worked on a hoop, it is more suitable for fine yarn and thin rag hooking. Your hoop can be attached quite easily to an improvised short base for lap work or a taller stand for seated work. This allows the free use of both hands.

Some frames have toothed grippers which facilitate the quick mounting, shifting and removal of the backing. Small, portable models (like the Puritan) can be used on the lap or on table-top. A larger frame can be mounted on saw horses and fitted with spikes (like wall-

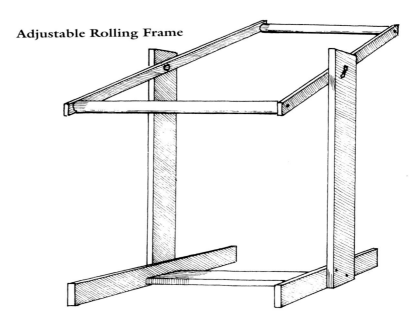

Adjustable Rolling Frame

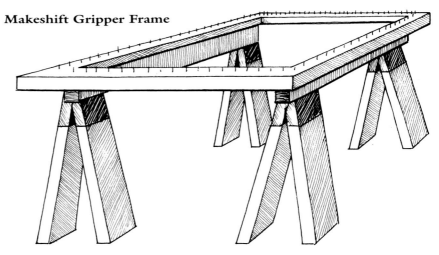

Makeshift Gripper Frame

to-wall carpet installation strips). Avoid the hazard of the spikes by covering them with masking tape or wood strips.

A more comfortable large frame can be constructed from wood in a free-standing fashion. Reinforced with metal L-brackets, it can be either fixed or adjustable with hinges at the base and locking wing nuts through slotted supports.

A most versatile large design is the adjustable rolling frame. The frame swivels to allow access to either surface of a rug. The horizontal members of the frame are large dowels with locking wing nuts, around which great lengths of backing can be wound.

Large Standing Frame

Basic Lap Frame

Puritan Frame

Lap Hoop Frame

Standing Hoop Frame

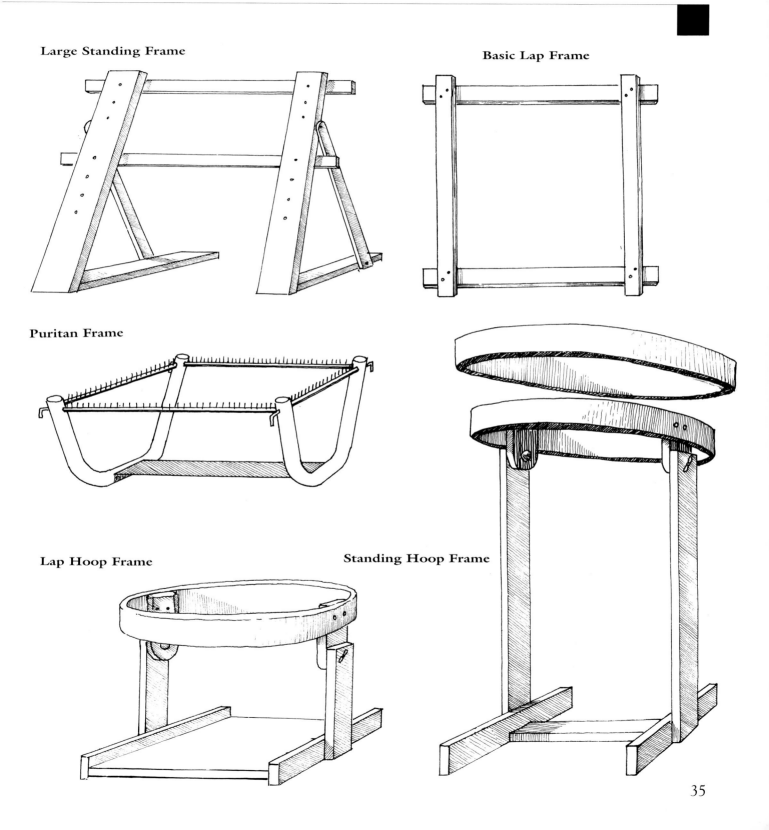

MISCELLANEOUS EQUIPMENT

A sharp pair of scissors with 8 to 10 inch blades is all you need to cut fabric strips for hooking. In time, you may choose to invest in a machine cutter which will enable you to cut strips far more quickly and accurately.

Machine cutters (like the Fraser, Bliss or Rigby models) usually clamp onto a table and are operated with a hand crank. Interchangeable cutter wheels produce several strips at a time and in widths that vary from 3/32 to 2 inches. There are also some less expensive hand-held cutters (like Olfa and Strip-It), but they are less accurate and efficient, and will not cut strips less than 1/4 inch.

A smaller pair of sharp scissors with 3 to 4 inch blades (possibly with curved handles) is ideal for trimming the tails off loops and fine detailing. A felt tip marking pen is needed to trace patterns onto backing. Rulers and tape measures come in handy. Upholstery-type T-pins can be useful to hold yarns or excess backing material in place.

Machine Cutter

FOUNDATIONS

The most commonly used material for backing is burlap. The inexpensive, looser weave (10 to 10-1/2 ounce variety) is preferable for primitive hooking, and comes in 3 or 4 foot widths. Be sure to inspect the burlap you buy for breaks in the fiber, as these will leave holes in your finished rug. A tighter weave burlap is suitable for traditional hooking.

The next most common option is cotton monk's cloth. Although its tighter weave and pliable texture may present more of a challenge to the novice hooker than burlap, it is preferred by many for its durability.

Other backing options include linen, heavy loose-weave cotton, and open-weave synthetics. If the weave is too tight for the width of strip you are hooking, skip over one or more holes with each loop. The main criteria for backing materials are loose weave, strength and non-elasticity.

Once you have chosen a pattern and a suitable piece of backing, it must be prepared for mounting on a frame. To allow for the finish binding, cut the backing with a 2 or 3 inch margin around the pattern edges. Various methods can be used to prevent the edges from raveling, and depend on the type of stress applied to the fabric during mounting on the frame. Masking tape folded around the edges will suffice in low stress. Painting a one-inch band of diluted white glue along the outer edge is another option. Zigzag stitching on a sewing machine works well, and if you will be lacing the backing to a large frame, folding and stitching a hem is advisable.

The methods of attaching the backing to a frame vary according to the frame and the size of the piece. The goal is always to stretch the backing tautly and evenly, preferably after you have transferred the pattern onto the fabric. Small pieces can be fastened around wooden lap frames with thumb tacks. Frames with gripper teeth make mounting quick and easy. When hooking larger pieces on a hoop, the thickness of the pile may strain inside the hoop as the work progresses. You can compensate for this by replacing the screw on the outer hoop with a longer one, allowing for expansion. As with any needlework, a rug should not be left in the hoop when you are not working on it. If your backing fits inside one of the big freestanding frames, you'll need to lace it in, not unlike a trampoline. Work your way around the whole piece with one length of strong string (like mason's twine) using a large yarn needle, adjusting for even tautness. If your piece is larger than the frame, wrap the edges over the frame and lace them together from behind. If you have an adjustable rolling frame, the shorter edges of a long piece can be tacked onto each of the dowels and rolled back and forth like a scroll.

WOOLGATHERING

Early rugs were often made from any old clothing that could no longer be recycled for further use. Mother's aprons and Sally's dresses passed down from an older sister were all fair game. The fabric was often cotton and, of course, would already have its unique shading from years of use. Today, 100% wool is preferred for several reasons. Anyone who has ever owned a woolen garment can appreciate its durability. Also, wool is an easy fabric to hand-dye. Old clothing remains an excellent source of wool to include in your rug. It costs nothing and is satisfying to see strips of your daughter's coat or your father's Sunday trousers in your rug. However, any wool that has been stored for long periods of time may have been prone to damage. Cut a strip of the old wool and see if it pulls apart, or test it by hooking it through a scrap of burlap.

Medium weight wool is best for hooking, such as 11-13 oz. tightly woven wool. The tighter the weave, the thinner the strip can be cut. Looser weaves can be used for wider strips, but should be preshrunk and matted. Plaids, herringbones, tweeds, heathers, stripes and checks make particularly interesting designs as they are hooked, and should not be overlooked. Blankets are generally too heavy for hooking.

Scavenging for choice woolens can take you to rummage sales, thrift shops, and clearance sales at clothing or fabric stores. Mail order houses sell second quality, mill ends and remnants by the yard or by the pound at reduced prices. You can also purchase pre-dyed, color gradated swatches of wool, as shown on page 49, from several specialty suppliers (see Acknowledgements). A rule of thumb for ordering the correct amount of wool of any given color, is to measure the surface area of that color zone in your pattern and multiply it by four. For traditional and contemporary style hooking, you may also want to consider yarns.

ALTERNATIVE MATERIALS

Whether you choose to embellish a traditional piece by hooking in a bit of satin ribbon or metallic thread, or plunge headlong into the exciting new contemporary approach to hooking, you should allow yourself the creative freedom to experiment with unconventional materials and techniques.

As wonderful as wool is, strips can also be cut from velours (cross-grain), organdy (straight-grain), satin (bias- and straight-cut), terry cloth, suede cloth, various knits, etc. Some materials will curl nicely into cords when pulled as strips.

Try hooking with all sorts of ribbons, raffias (natural and synthetic), papers, mylar, acrylics, plastics, monofilament nylon, metallic yarns and threads. See how various weights of woolen yarns hooked in different size loops create wonderful textural effects—not to mention unusual yarns made of mohair, chenille and bouclé. In fact, you can ply your own yarn by mixing various

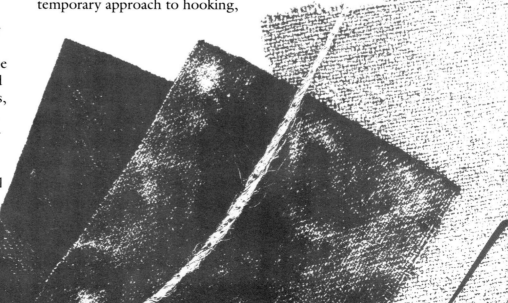

strands of yarns, threads and other fibers such as cotton, linen, rayon and synthetics.

You can also sculpt hooked loops into three-dimensional forms. First, hook an outline with yarn (woolen or synthetic), then fill it in densely with high loops until it is tightly packed and firm. Using small scissors, clip off the loop tops, then continue sculpting the pile into the desired shape.

Interesting shag textures can be created with small patches of fabric. Inserting a chopstick into the center of squares or circles of cloth to form little tents and then poking them through the backing produces tufting on one side and billows on the other. Both effects are usable, and can be secured with glue. The tufted side can be clipped different ways to make a shag.

Any number of materials can be hooked or otherwise fastened into the backing. Not to be overlooked are metal wires, springs, foils, washers and other hardware…virtually all sorts of raw materials and found objects.

PREPARING STRIPS

In order to prepare woolens for conventional hooking strips, they must first be cleaned—especially old recycled garments. Wash them with standard detergent in warm water in the machine or by hand. They can be dried by machine on normal setting. The fabric shrinkage will tighten the weave for strength.

Next, remove all buttons, button-holes, zippers, pockets, skirt bands, collars, cuffs, facings, etc. Cut out darts, tucks, pleats, mothholes, weak spots, and cut open all seams.

Sort the pieces by color and/or texture. Stack each grouping flat (to prevent wrinkling), then roll it into a bundle.

These can be stored in sealed plastic bags for later use. You may want to keep small color samples and record the amounts of each for future project reference.

Unless you plan to dye your wool, the next step is cutting it into strips of appropriate width. For primitive hooking, a good shortcut is to first tear the wool into strips 5/8-3/4 inches wide, then cut them down the middle with large shears. Length of strips can vary, but are usually about a foot or longer. All strips must be cut on the straight of the weave. Keep your scissors sharp.

For cutting narrower strips used in traditional hooking, it is advisable to use a machine cutter, but it is a matter of your own patience and precision. The cutting wheels that are made for machine cutters come in standard widths, usually designated #3 (3/32"), #4 (1/8"), #5 (5/32"), #6 (3/16"), #7 (7/32"), & #8 (1/4"). A popular width for many traditional hookers is 3/32", although 1/8" is usually quite sufficient for most designs. It will be easier to cut along the straight of the weave if you periodically snip and tear the wool, then use the torn edge as a guide when passing it through the machine.

Dyeing

Primitive hooked rugs often have muted colors. If the wool scraps you have collected or bought appear too bright for your rug, you may want to consider overdyeing your wool. A light dyebath of "khaki drab" dye will tone down most bright colors. Another method of overdyeing uses the complementary color of whatever color wool you wish to mute. You may also choose to dye your wool unevenly to mottle it for a rich antique look. Major brands of dye are sold in 1/3 oz. packages which are perfect for dyeing smaller amounts of wool. You should also feel free to experiment with natural dyes.

Dyeing for primitive hooking is actually quite simple, and requires common household items: an enamel pot, measuring spoons, measuring cups, and white vinegar. However, do not dye in pans you intend to use for cooking. After cleaning and cutting the wool into manageable pieces, soak it in warm water for a minimum of 2 hours, or overnight if possible. Place the desired amount of dye in a measuring cup and add a small amount of hot water to make a paste. Add additional hot water and stir, making sure all dye is dissolved before it is placed in the dye pot. Add presoaked wool to the simmering dye mixture. After the wool has simmered in the dye for 15 minutes, add 1/4 cup of vinegar to set the dye, and continue to simmer for 30 more minutes. (Remember, wet wool appears darker than dry wool.) Let the wool cool in the pot, then rinse it in your washing machine. Dry it in your machine or on the line. Primitive rugs do not have the intricately planned shading of traditional rugs. For this reason, mottled wool or wool that has light and medium values lends itself nicely to primitive hooking and helps give the rugs their characteristic, antique look. The degree of mottling in a piece of wool depends on how much wool was dyed together. The less room the wool has to move in the pot, the more mottled the final produce will be. Conversely, consistent stirring while the wool is simmering will result in very uniform dyeing. So for primitive dyeing, it is best to stir very little.

These days, traditional rug hooking has advanced to a point where there are lots of sophisticated things going on with color and dyeing. However, if you happen to have no or very little experience with either rug hooking or dyeing, you may want to consider these two basic approaches to dyeing.

The first is to dye what you need with the help of formulas. If this appeals to you, there are hundreds of formulas available to rug hookers through booklets that can be readily purchased. Most are written for a specific dye (such as Cushing or Proacid). The second approach is to create your own colors as you go by mixing them by eye, adding different amounts depending on whether you want a darker, brighter or duller color. Both approaches are very effective, depending on what you are trying to accomplish.

Simply speaking, all colors can be mixed from red, yellow, blue and black. With practice we learn to mix red and yellow to get orange, red and blue to get purple, and yellow and blue to get green. These are the primary and secondary colors. As rug hookers we want to know how to mix all colors including bright ones, dull ones, light ones and dark ones. Therefore, we need to understand some additional things about color. For instance, if a color you are trying to dye is too bright, add a bit of its complement. (Complementary colors are those that lie opposite each other on the color wheel.) You can change bright orange wool into a beautiful rust by adding its complement, blue. Keep in mind that every time you add more complementary color, the results will be darker as well as duller.

Color is a very exciting part of rug hooking. You can accomplish a great deal by reading and experimenting on your own, or by taking a class.

DESIGNS

There are ready-made patterns in this and other books that you can transfer onto your backing using the grid method. You can also order patterns already printed on your choice of backing through catalogs, as well as kits complete with materials. But after you have mastered some of the projects in this book, you may want to try your hand at the design process. This will involve drawing a pattern, transferring it onto your backing, and planning the colors.

The inspiration for a design can come from anywhere, and gives you the opportunity to express your ideas and aesthetics. Your pattern may evolve out of the abstract: a feeling, a memory, or a mood. It might depict an event or story. You may want to translate concrete images into your rug, such as your house, a favorite pet, a family portrait, or a primitive drawing by your child. Many rug hookers draw on other media for design motifs: tapestries, quilts, samplers, wallpapers, china patterns, architectural styles, paintings, etc. Your choice of pattern may also be determined by a specific place your rug or wall hanging will be displayed.

If you are comfortable with sketching, you may opt to draw your pattern directly on the backing. Start lightly with a soft pencil, then trace over the finished lines with a permanent

Several antique border patterns, from W. W. Kent's book, *The Hooked Rug.*

marker. However, if you are more comfortable refining your pattern first on paper, there are several methods of transferring it to the backing.

If your paper pattern is to scale, you can transfer it with tracing paper and a transfer pencil (available at art supply stores). Draw your design on the tracing paper using a regular pencil. Turn the paper over and trace the outline of your subject with the transfer pencil. Place a towel over the area where the pattern is to be transferred. Aluminum foil placed over the towel will help to transfer the heat back up to the backing when ironed. This aids in making the design clearer. Place a hot dry iron over the transfer paper, being sure to apply heat to all the areas of the design. Once the design has been imprinted, it is wise to go over the lines with a permanent marker, as it may fade over time. (Carbon paper is another option, but may need to be used piecemeal.)

Designs can also be projected in slide form through a projector. You can photograph any image, or may already have a slide—or a composite of slides—you want to use. The image can be projected onto tracing paper, or directly on your backing (preferably white fabric like monk's cloth). Adjust the distance of the projector from the wall where it is mounted to achieve the proper scale. If tracing the image onto tracing paper, the transfer pencil method can be used.

For the patterns in this book and elsewhere, you can utilize the grid method. This will enable you to transfer a pattern of any size onto any size backing. Lightly sketch a grid with the same number of squares as your pattern onto the backing. (If you want to alter the proportions, stretch or compress these squares into rectangles to fit your preferred dimensions.) Lightly

Two fine examples of contrasting color plans interpreting the "Royalty" rug pattern, hooked by Lucile Keeler and Verna Howland, from Pearl McGown's book, *The Lore and Lure of Hooked Rugs*.

sketch the outlines that appear in each square of your pattern onto the corresponding squares on the backing, then go over the outlines with a permanent marker.

The last primary design element, besides the possible variation of texture, is color. You are free to invent your own color plan for any pattern, although certain rules of design will prove useful. A primary consideration is achieving effective contrast and balance between light and dark areas of your design. It's a good idea to first decide if you want

the background to be light or dark. The featured motif can then occupy the opposite end of the spectrum. The fine shading of traditional hooking utilizes the subtle gradation of hue to great effect. Creating three-dimensional images requires an awareness of light source and shadow. Personal taste and a sense of your desired effect will guide you, ultimately.

As you choose your colors, certain complex areas of your pattern should be diagramed. This record of your color plan

will serve your memory as you hook. You can see examples of this device in the more advanced projects in this book, where colors are keyed using numbers or letters to show both the placement and direction of hooking each shade.

Having completed your color plan, you should gather all the color samples of your wool and place them on their pattern areas. This will allow you to check their compatibility. Don't be discouraged if this turns into a trial and error procedure.

HOOKING TECHNIQUES

The actual process of hooking is quite simply a matter of pulling strips of fabric through a backing to make the loops which form the pile. Traditional hooking differs from primitive hooking primarily because the strips are narrower, the loops are tighter, and the pattern designs are more intricate—otherwise, the same procedures apply.

After you have read these instructions, you should practice on a scrap of burlap to get the feel of it. Before starting a project, find a well lit area with a comfortable chair, and gather together your frame, hook, scissors, and all your materials.

The hook is held in the right hand above the backing while the strip is held between the thumb and the forefinger underneath, unless you are left handed. Insert the hook through a hole in the backing and catch the end of the strip, pulling it up through the backing to the top to a length of about 1/2 - 1 inch. (See Figure 1.) This "tail" will be trimmed off even with the pile later. Insert the hook through the next hole and pull the first loop to the top. Continue pulling loops (see Figure 2) until about 1/2 - 1 inch of the strip remains, then pull that tail to the top. To hook the next strip, pull its tail through the same hole

you just finished, and proceed. (See Figure 3.)

The height of the loops will depend on your style of hooking and the thickness of your strips. Generally, the loops should be as high as they are wide, i.e. 1/4" strips are pulled into 1/4" high loops. This can be varied somewhat for textural effect, especially

with alternative materials. In any case, the goal is to create a firm pile. The loops should touch, but not crush each other. This means that you will not always hook through every hole in the backing mesh, but adjust the spacing of the loops as necessary to achieve a good pile. If the loops are packed too tightly they

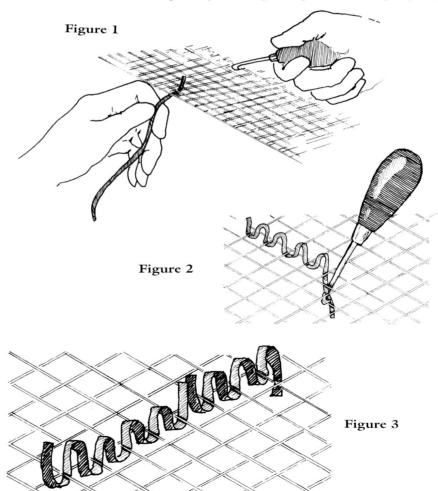

Figure 1

Figure 2

Figure 3

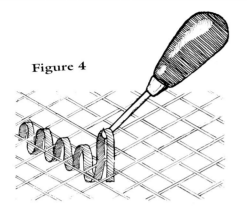

Figure 4

Figure 5

will strain the backing, and if too loosely the rug will wear poorly.

As you are pulling loops, you may find that the edges of a loop top come up crimped or crooked—especially with wider strips. To remedy this, pull the loop twice as high, straighten it with your hook, then pull it back from underneath to its proper height. (See Figure 4.)

As you insert your hook through each hole in the backing, press the smooth edge of the shaft against the mesh a little. This will enlarge the hole a bit so that the barb of the hook won't catch on the mesh as you pull the loop through. If you find that you are pulling out each previous loop as you pull up a new one, twist the hook slightly away from you as you pull up each loop.

Practice hooking in straight lines, curves, then in little circles. Fill in the circles with concentric circles or a spiral. The top surface should be flush and the loops all evenly spaced. After hooking your rug, check for gaps and hook small strips to fill them.

The underside of the backing should feel smooth with no lumps, twists, or loose tails. The tails on the top surface can be periodically trimmed flush with the pile using small scissors. Be careful not to clip any adjoining loops, and cut them straight across. Remember, this is a hand craft, so your finished project will not look machine made. Part of the charm of rug hooking is that each rug has its own unique look and history.

When you begin your rug, start by outlining the figures in the center of the pattern. Use the color that will be filling each shape (or possibly a shade darker) to outline, then fill them in. Follow the contours of each outline as you fill them, or vary the direction of the lines to create interior patterns, but don't jump rows or cross back over. If there is a border to your pattern, it should be hooked next. The background is done last.

Since the colors of the background are usually monotone, the patterns created by the direction of hooking become more important. By exploiting this special feature of hooking, you can add interest, dimension, and a sense of movement to any background with shifting contours of line as well as subtle variations in color. The direction of hooking can be straight, wavy, curled, geometric, random—almost anything. (See Figure 5.)

In some areas of your pattern, it will not be possible to begin a new strip where you ended the last one. In these places, start the new strip as close as possible to another loop, and leave the tails until the surrounding areas are filled in. Also, when hooking diagonally across the weave of the backing, take care to maintain a consistent spacing of loops. When hooking the very corners and edges of the rug, hook the loops a little bit more closely to stand up to wear.

Concerning the different approaches to traditional technique, some of these subtle variations will become evident with the later projects in this book.

BINDING & FINISHING

Regardless of what type of hooked piece you are finishing, the most important step is the pressing you do before you begin any of the other steps such as binding, mounting, etc. Place a very damp cloth on the backing side and press with a hot iron. Check to see that you are smoothing out any lumps. Turn the piece over and press the top side in the same manner, but more gently. Allow the piece to dry flat at least 12 hours, or longer in high humidity.

One of several possible methods of binding a rug is begun before you start to hook. You will need a length of twilled binding tape 1-1/4" wide in a color that is compatible with your rug. You can also dye white tape along with your wool, but in either case you must preshrink the tape before sewing it on. Allow about 4" shrinkage per yard.

Machine stitch two rows or a zigzag 1" outside the edge of your pattern. Lay the tape on the backing just inside the edge of the pattern, and machine stitch 1/8" from this edge all the way around (see diagram). Begin and end the tape in the center of a side—never at the corner—and overlap the ends about 3/4". The tape can then be basted temporarily to the backing out of the way. Hook at least two parallel rows as close to the tape as possible.

When you're ready to bind the rug, cut the backing just outside the 1" margin of stitching, then fold the tape and the backing along an imaginary line 1/4" outside the edge of hooking. Miter the corners, and hand stitch the tape to the underside of the rug using heavy-duty thread.

A variation of this method can be used *after* you have hooked

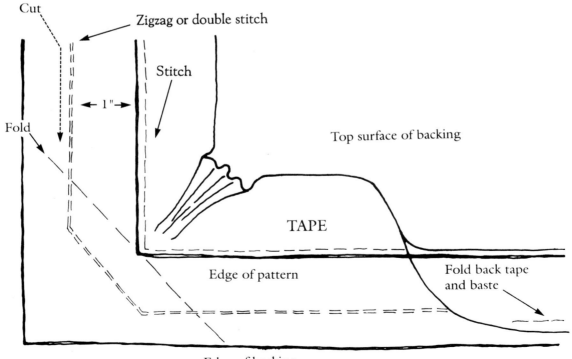

Cut

Zigzag or double stitch

Stitch

← 1" →

Fold

Top surface of backing

TAPE

Edge of pattern

Fold back tape and baste

Edge of backing

46

the rug. Be sure you have hooked at least two parallel rows right up to the edge of the pattern. Place the tape on the top side right up against the hooking, and sew this edge by hand to the backing with heavy-duty, color-matched thread. Trim the backing, fold and hem in the same manner as the first method.

Another method involves whipping the edge of the rug, which prevents the backing from fraying. Use a cable cord such as piping sold for upholstery or pillows. Place the cord under the edge of the backing, just next to the outer row of hooking. Roll the edge of the backing around the cord to the underside, and baste it in place. Grade the strands of the cord where they meet to splice an overlap of about 2 inches. (The cord can be omitted in smaller rugs.)

Whipstitch the edge, around the cord, with wool yarn by inserting the needle from the back to the front, making sure that you go in the same row of holes in the backing as your last row of hooked loops. You will find that it is necessary to whip in almost every hole in the backing in order to cover it. Do not leave knots showing. Pull them in to the corded edge. When you come to the end of your yarn, pull it in as well. Fifteen yards of wool will whip 12 inches of edging, using a double strand.

Trim the excess backing

underneath to a 1" margin and fell to the rug using an overcast stitch or feather stitch, making sure that you catch the backing rather than just the back of your hooked loops. Miter the corners by folding neatly to minimize bulk. Then seal the area by sewing both edges of 1-1/4" twill binding tape to the backing, just inside the whipped edge.

Binding circular or oval rugs presents more of a challenge. Always work on a flat surface to avoid distorting the shape. Binding with regular tape is more difficult because of all the pleating that occurs around curves. It is preferable to make your own tape by cutting strong cotton or wool on the bias to conform to your edge.

In addition to binding the edge, you may want to finish the backing with glue. This is mostly done for small pieces like welcome mats, table mats, hot pads, ornamental pieces, or rugs that incorporate alternative materials. Latex is ideal for this purpose, creating a durable, skidproof coating, and can be purchased at most carpet supply outlets. After clipping and vacuum cleaning the underside, deposit a glob of undiluted latex in the center of the backing, and spread it evenly over the surface with a disposable knife or spatula. Be careful not to oversaturate the fabric, and work in a ventilated area. Diluted white glue can also be used, but

becomes brittle after drying. A third option involves cutting a piece of wool or felt the same size as your hooked piece, applying spray glue to one surface and to the hooked backing, then sticking them together. However, most rugs will not require any sort of glue finishing.

If you intend your hooked piece only for display as a wall hanging, you might consider a full lining rather than binding tape. The lining fabric should coordinate with the piece, and can be sewn right to the edges of the backing, which has been turned under and hemmed. A strip of wooden lath across the top edge, or eyelets, or a large dowel through loops, or any number of methods can be used for mounting. A heavy rod or drapery weights at the bottom will also help maintain its shape. Other wall pieces can be mounted on a board and framed like an oil painting.

For a final touch, sew a label on to the backing of your piece. Even though you may have incorporated your name, your initials, or the year into the hooked design, a label can include more detailed information. Record your full name, the title of the piece or pattern, the date and place where it was hooked, and the designer's name.

FRINGE

Certain rugs, such as orientals and even some contemporaries, look much better with fringe on them. A standard approach is to whip the long edges of the rectangle (as explained before) and add fringe to the shorter ends.

Although fringe can be purchased ready made, you can make it yourself using strong yarns, cotton cord, or other plied fibers. It can be dyed to coordinate with the rug, or left natural. If you plan to add fringe using this first method, be sure you have machine stitched (two tight rows or zigzag) the backing 1" outside the pattern before hooking, to prevent fraying.

After hooking, fold the backing underneath, but leave about 1/8" of it extending beyond the pattern. With a darning needle, make a row of blanket stitches across this edge. If you crochet, you can substitute two rows of single crochet across the edge. Next, cut a good quantity of 5" lengths of fringe material. (A quick method is to wind it around a 2-1/2" strip of cardboard, then cut it once down one side.) Fold each strip in half, hook it through each stitch along the edge, and tie it off with a cow hitch. (See Figure 1.) Then trim off excess backing, just past the zigzag stitch, and bind it all the way around with 1-1/4" twill tape.

There is an easier, less refined fringe method that can work with coarse backings like heavy burlap. Before hooking, simply machine stitch several tight rows back and forth on the fringe edge of the backing, just outside the pattern. Then remove the fibers parallel to the edge, one by one. They can be left as is, or knotted in groups. (See Figure 2.)

MAINTENANCE & REPAIR

Some hazards to your rug are avoidable. The beauty of a hooked rug is enhanced to a degree by walking on it, but avoid high traffic areas that will soil and strain its fibers past their limits. A thin rubber pad placed under your rug will help extend its life. It should be cut 1/2" inside the edges of the rug.

Rugs last longer when they are cleaned periodically. Gentle vacuuming works best for long-term maintenance. Use a canister or tank-type machine and an upholstery attachment—never a brush-action unit. Let the suction do the work, and vacuum the underside as well. Rugs should occasionally be aired outdoors, especially on damp, foggy days which can make burlap backings less brittle. Rugs can be lightly cleaned by shaking them, but only *gently,* to avoid weakening the backing. After becoming

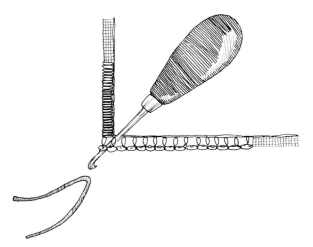

Figure 1

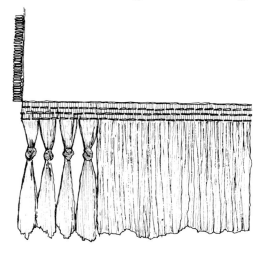

Figure 2

overly soiled, they can be cleaned commercially, but this should be avoided as much as possible.

Accidental stains should be removed immediately. You can treat your newly finished rug with several applications of a spray-on repellent (like Scotch-gard™) as a preventive measure. When liquid stains occur, blot them firmly with towels. If necessary, you can then sponge the area gently with cold water. If the stain persists, use a mild solution of cold water and white vinegar or household ammonia. Soaps and detergents should be avoided because the suds are difficult to remove. Also avoid commercial rug cleaners which may actually set the stain and damage fibers with harsh chemicals. Solid stains, such as food and dirt, should be gently lifted out of the fibers rather than rubbed further in. Try spot vacuuming as you loosen the particles with a knife. Hand washing an entire rug is a delicate process that should be avoided since it weakens the backing and may actually damage the piece.

When you roll up a rug to transport or store it, roll so that the top surface faces outward. This prevents the backing from stretching and weakening. If it is to be stored a while, it can be wrapped in plastic or heavy paper (preferably acid-free) with a few moth balls. Don't store a rug wrapped in plastic where it is subject to sunlight or excessive heat, as moisture will collect and cause mildew.

Woolen Color Swatches

Structural damage can be repaired in a number of ways. If your pet cat claws up a few loops, you simply hook them back in place or hook new ones to match. If the backing develops a weak spot or is accidentally cut, unravel some threads from a scrap of matching backing material and darn them back into the weave. This can also be reinforced with a little diluted white glue after the loops have been hooked back.

For larger holes in the backing, sew on a patch of monk's cloth by hand. Also stitch down the frayed area of the backing to the patch from the top side of the rug. Then rehook the area with matching strips. If a rug has developed widespread breaks in the backing due to age, it is time for a new backing. Use monk's cloth, and cut it slightly larger than the rug so that the edges can be turned under when sewing it to the rug's edge. Stitch the monk's cloth to the backing at various intervals to hold them together evenly. Wherever there are breaks, remove the loose loops, stitch the frayed area to the monk's cloth, and rehook as with smaller patch-work. If the edges of an old rug are particularly worn, remove the binding along with all the loose loops, attach a whole new backing, stitch down the frayed edges of backing, then rehook and rebind the piece.

Heart and Hands (12-1/2" x 20"), hooked and designed by Beth Sekerka.

This classic primitive design is an excellent candidate for your first attempt at rug hooking. The standard 1/4" strips can be hand cut from wool scraps and used as is, or overdyed. The background in this rug was made of various scraps and overdyed with "antique black" for a mottled effect. You may want to substitute your own color plan, but the amounts of each color used here are:

3-1/2 oz. red
3 oz. beige
9-1/2 oz. black

Notice how effectively each area is contoured by the direction of hooking. Let your hands follow your heart as you hook this rug.

This charming primitive is quite typical of colonial American rugs, both in its motif and distinctive shape. It also affords the beginning rug hooker with an opportunity to hook straight geometrics as well as curved lines.

The background of this rug was hooked with various scraps, overdyed with "antique black." The strips are cut in 1/4" widths. The amounts of the various colors you will need are:

2 oz. white
1 oz. gold
1/4 oz. blue
1 oz. red
1 oz. gray
6-1/2 oz. background

Take care when binding the curved edge of this rug to avoid puckering and pleating of the binding tape.

Small Homestead (12-1/4" x 17-3/4"), hooked by Beth McCastland, designed by Beth Sekerka.

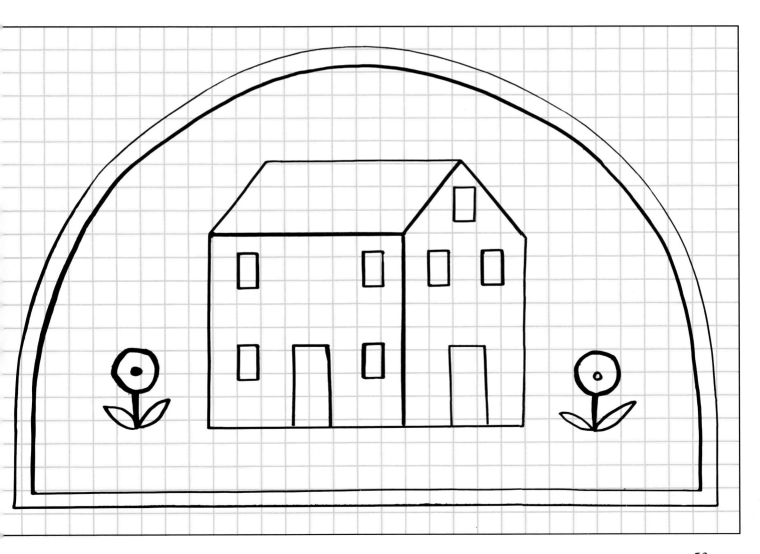

This primitive teddy bear pattern is very simple, so the wools used to hook it should be exciting.

If you happen to have an old camel skirt you don't care for anymore, you can use it now. Rust, mummy brown, gray, spice brown or any reddish brown will give the camel wool nice spots for a bear. Make sure the wool is crumpled in the dye pan so that there are many ridges and valleys. This wrinkling of the wool will cause it to dye in a hit 'n' miss fashion. Spoon these various dyes you have chosen and spot the camel wool. Using kosher salt, salt the wool, add water—on the side of the wool so the spots don't wash out—and cover with tin foil. Place in a 350 degree oven for one hour. Be careful when you take the pan out. Cool first. Do not take the foil off the top immediately as the steam you release from the pan may be enough to cause burns.

If you have more camel skirt material, you can spot it in the same fashion to do the background. This time spot with red dyes, which are also dissolved in individual cups of boiling water. Once the reds have been spooned onto the camel wool, you can dissolve 1/4 teaspoon of black into one cup of boiling water and spoon some of this onto the wool. This will give strong black spots to make an effective background. You could also spot red wool to use for the background with green and black, also dissolving each dye in one cup of water.

A solid white bear could be hooked, and a tweed with a lot of color in it for the background. There are wonderful skirts of maroon, green, and camel

Caitlin's Toy (18-1/2" x
24-1/2"), hooked and
designed by Marie
Azzaro.

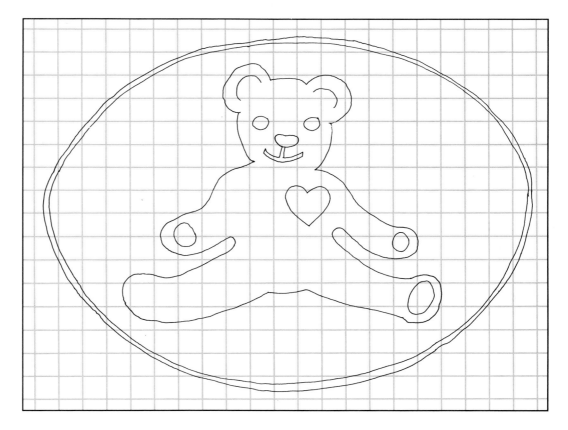

tweeds that would make a wonderful background
without any dyeing. A camel bear could be hooked
using a tweed background from a piece of fabric
that had a lot of interest. Striped wool hooked in
the north to south direction for the background
would be most effective behind a solid bear that
coordinated with the stripe.

This rug was originally designed for a beginning rug hooking class. It is very appropriate for the novice rug crafter because of its simple straight lines and primitive 1/4" strips.

The main thing to keep in mind when choosing your wool is the color values. You should plan to hook either light stars on a dark background, or dark stars on a light background.

Wool requirements can be limited to as few as three or four colors. It is also possible to hook this rug with all "as-is" wool, just as this rug was done. If you want an antique look, be sure to use lots of textured pieces like tweeds, herringbones, and checks. Using one accent color (like the red rust shown here) in small amounts will add "spark" to the finished piece.

When hooking the stars, start at each tip and work toward the center. This will help you achieve more pointed tips.

Twinkle Stars (18-1/2" x 24"),
hooked and designed by Kathy
Morton.

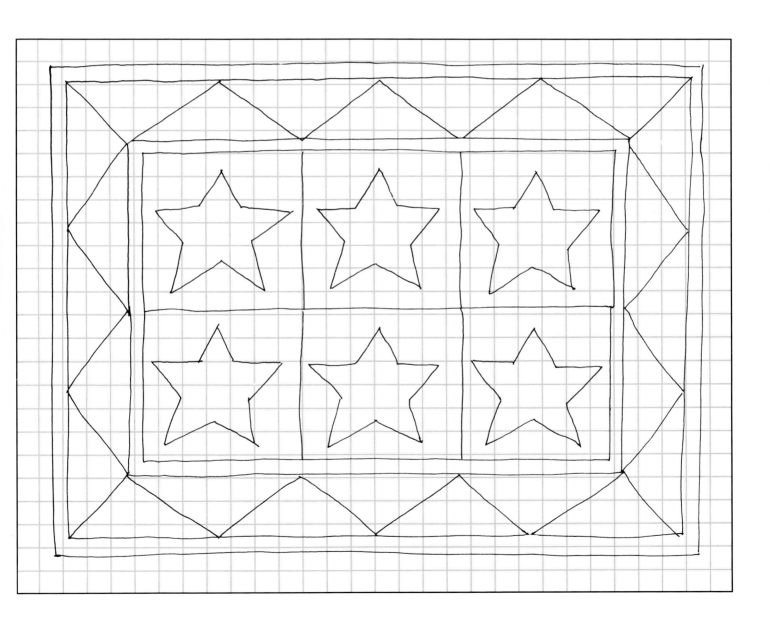

Window Shopping (24" x 40"), hooked and designed by **Marie Azzaro.**

This is the type of primitive that is simpler than it looks. It is a fun project because if you rummage around you may be able to do the whole pattern from small pieces of leftover woolens from sewing projects or old garments.

The sky was done with a camel colored wool that was used as is. All of the houses are tweeds that had some white in them. The red roof was a tweed that was overdyed in Egyptian red. The house with the cat in the window was a tweed that had some orange in it and was overdyed with some brown. Copenhagen blue dye was used to dye a tweed that ended up being the bottom house on the pattern. The ground was a textured piece of wool that was a light brown color but had flecks of dull red in it. This was used as is, and made a good ground cover. The stone walkway was this same ground wool, dyed in brown. A few pieces of gray herringbone overdyed with olive green made lovely trees. The ground cover dyed an even darker brown was used for the trunks of the trees and an outline for one of the houses. Note how bright the outline of the boy's hat is, and also how bright the girl's hair is next to the muted tones of the rest of the rug. The white dog is pure white and not muted with dye.

The border on this design is a herringbone dyed in brown to frame all the earth tones in the design. Once the wool has been selected for the ground of this pattern, you can start deciding on the colors of the houses which will sit on the ground color. Always remember to hook with colors that create definition in the pattern. Each house has a contrasting outline around it which strengthens the contrast between the color of the house and the background color. Stripes, checks, and tweeds are perfect elements for this pattern, and can be used to hook the entire design.

You may notice the smoke coming out of the chimneys is blowing in different directions. Taking such creative license is a good way to personalize your rugs and make them conversation pieces.

After hooking this good-size rug, you may want to experiment with shading in your next project, since the consecutive outlining in this design is only one step away. The strips are 1/4" wide.

The amounts of color used in this rug are:

8 oz. white
2-1/2 oz. light pink
2-1/2 oz. dark pink
16 oz. light blue/green
2-1/2 oz. taupe
3-1/2 oz. gold

3-1/2 oz. rust
2 oz. blue
1/2 oz. black
15-1/2 oz. dark green
2 oz. green (leaves)

If dyeing the wool yourself, notice how the mottled background adds interest and texture to the piece, and creates more of a dramatic contrast with the stark white of the swan. The colors of the border could be varied quite easily to complement your own decor.

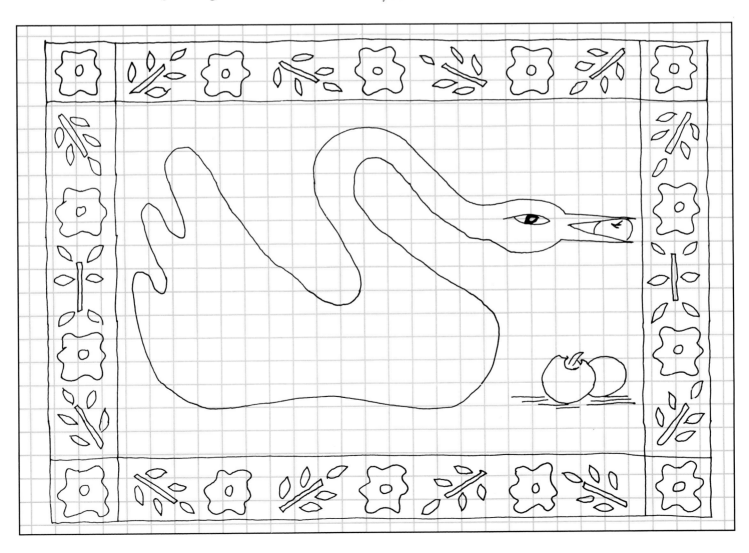

Long Neck Swan (26-1/2" x 34-1/2"), hooked by Beth Sekerka, designed by Marie Azzaro.

If you want your cat to have this striped effect, find or dye two or three colors in a close color range to hook texture into the animal. Hook the cat's body in the same direction as the fur would grow. You'll be amazed how much shading you can achieve with 1/4" strips.

For the background, search for a tweed or plaid wool that blends with your other rug colors. By doing this, the background is not flat, but has textural interest which does not overwhelm the cat. A large turquoise-gold plaid men's sport coat, size 44, yielded a grand amount of wool for this rug! Tweeds and plaids can also be overdyed to harmonize with your color scheme.

Tiger Cat (18" x 33"), **hooked and designed by Kathy Morton.**

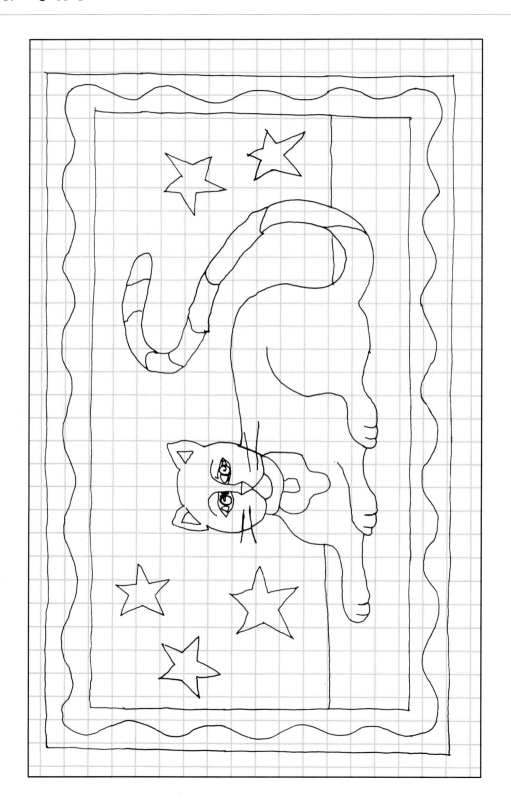

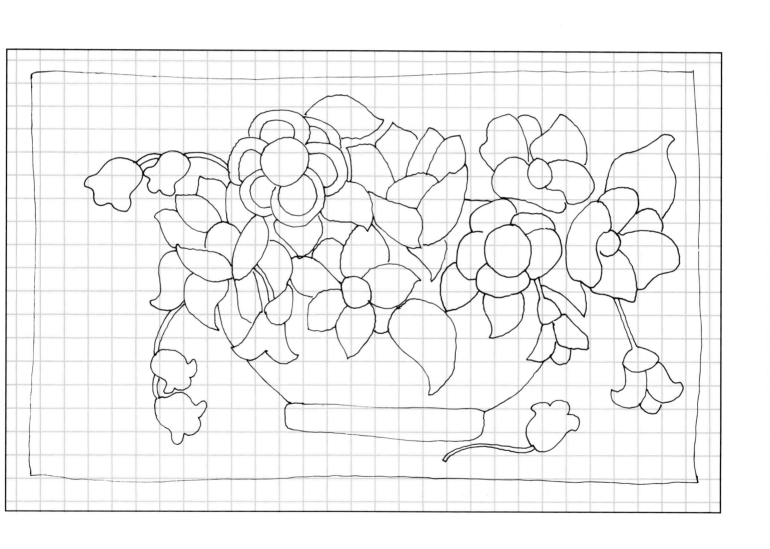

***Bernie's Pot* (23" x 35"), hooked by Andrew Graham from a Yankee Peddler design.**

This attractively shaded rug was hooked as a primitive, using the standard 1/4" strips. The technique used for shading is a simplified version of those employed in traditional hooking.

Basically, each shape is outlined and then filled in round and round with bands of different shades of similar color. This gives a sense of three-dimensional realism, but remains stylized in a primitive mode.

You may have difficulty finding this many colors "as is." But before you consider buying them pre-dyed, try collecting about three different light colors and overdye each one in progressively darker shades.

Notice how dramatically the subject stands out against the black background. Notice too how the background holds its own interest with mottled shades that are hooked in contours.

Squirrel with Berries (27" diameter), hooked and
designed by Kathy Morton.

SQUIRREL WITH BERRIES

This octagonal primitive is a fun shape to hook and won't present any special problems to the novice. The only thing to watch for is to miter each corner neatly when binding the finished rug.

When hooking the oak leaves, use colors that celebrate the turning of leaves in the fall. Keep a dark outline for the veins and the edges of the leaves so that the leaf shapes are crisp and do not fade into the background.

The background is much more interesting if it is not hooked in one flat color. Instead, use three values of one hue and mix them like a "tossed salad." This technique adds movement to the rug and gives it a more antique appearance.

To make the squirrel seem more alive, add a small, white, french knot to his eye.

THE PRAIRIE FOX

Generally, this primitive pattern is recommended for more experienced rug hookers. It is also rather large and more time consuming.

The ground and the sky around the fox were both spot-dyed with washes of greens, browns, and reds (colors that reappear in other portions of the rug). This technique adds color interest to the background without detracting from the main focus, the fox.

You can achieve luminescence in the leaves and acorns by hooking in small amounts of very light colors at the tips of the shapes where they touch the dark brown border. This dab of "sparkle" is the same technique painters use when adding small dots of white to bring life to their paintings.

The dark brown in the border is hooked in curved lines to repeat the shapes of the leaves and tendrils in the design. Straight-line hooking would have flattened out these shapes.

The Prairie Fox (27" x 54"), **hooked and designed by Kathy Morton.**

Cabin Repeat (8" x 8"), hooked by Nancy Miller,
designed by Jane Flynn.

CABIN REPEAT

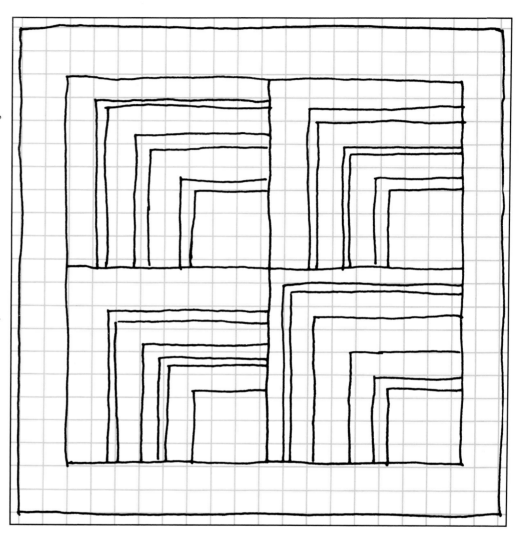

Patterned after the popular Log Cabin Repeat quilt design, this piece can be developed in primitive, traditional or contemporary style. It is an excellent starter piece, since it is small and is hooked in straight lines. The project shown here was hooked using a variety of width strips (3/32", 4/32", and 6/32") of pastel wool yardage. It also includes wool yarn, cotton transitional colored yarn, and metallic threads. By combining materials and different width strips, you can experiment to find what materials and size of cut strips you are most comfortable with before going on to a larger project. If you are an experienced hooker, this is an excellent piece for using leftover strips from past projects.

To begin, go through your hooking bag, yarn bin, sewing basket and ribbon box, collecting leftover materials. Experiment with anything that might be hookable. If you can hook it, use it! The combination of wool strips, yarns, ribbons, raw fleece, and other materials adds texture and interest to this piece. When hooking a rug that will be walked on, use alternative materials sparingly as some materials do not wear well as well as hooked strips, and may tend to pull out more easily.

First hook the dividing line between the four blocks. Next, hook the line surrounding the four blocks. These lines will guide you as to where to start and end the rows within each block. Hook the lower corner block of one of the squares, and finish the complete square before moving on to the next. When the four blocks are completed, add a border if you decide to include one.

Hook some of the rows higher than others. Pull some rows very high and cut the tops of the loops off with scissors to give a shag effect. Hook some of the rows with alternating high and low loops, or alternating two low and one high loop. Play with this piece, experiment and have fun. You can use this piece for a wall hanging, table mat, pillow or trivet.

This pattern comes alive with the multi-color scraps that accumulate as leftovers from other projects. The more varied the colors, the greater the appeal.

The approach to this design is quite simple. The piece is held together visually by hooking the center, the spokes and the outer border all in one color. The pie-shaped wedges are then filled in with parallel rows of alternating colors.

The strips can be any width in any given row, although the height of the loop should not vary too much. This design approach can also be translated into other patterns, such as squares or the log cabin repeat used in the last project.

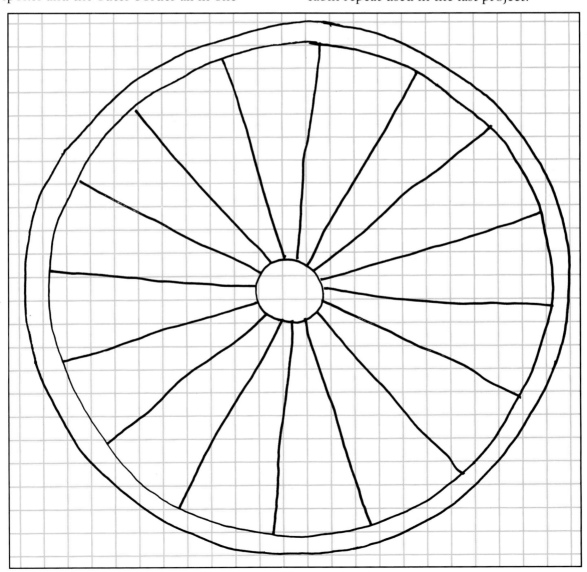

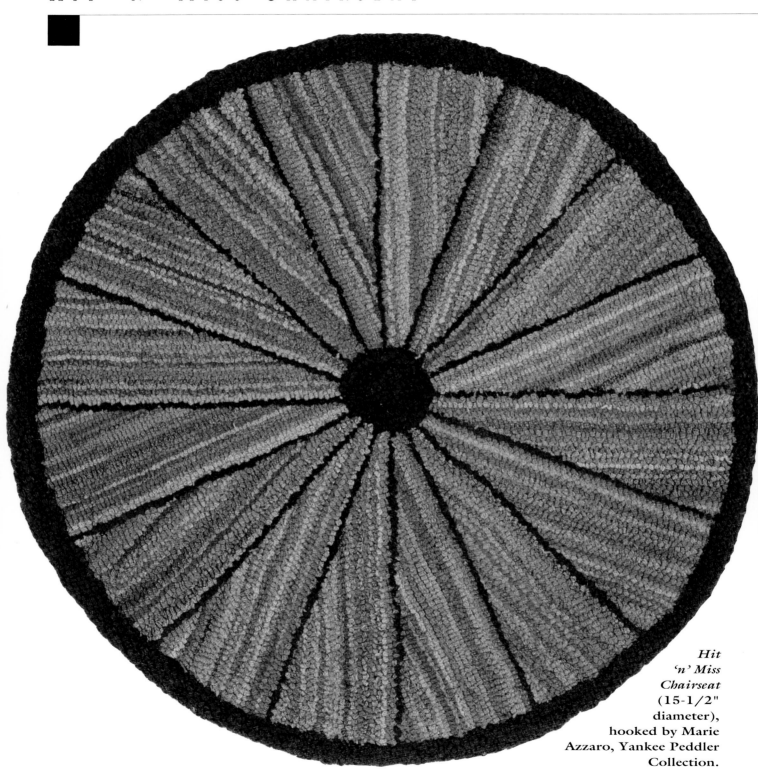

Hit 'n' Miss Chairseat **(15-1/2" diameter), hooked by Marie Azzaro, Yankee Peddler Collection.**

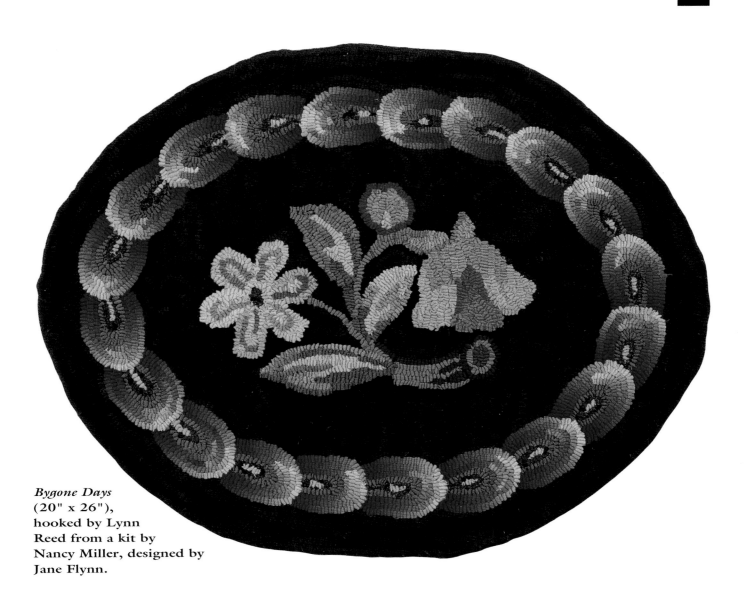

Bygone Days
(20" x 26"),
hooked by Lynn
Reed from a kit by
Nancy Miller, designed by
Jane Flynn.

This is a good design for a first floral rug, since it is relatively small and has much flexibility in style. It can be hooked with primitive or traditional methods using any cutter width or with hand-cut strips.

The rug in this photo demonstrates simple shading techniques using four value swatches of turquoise green and spice brown, six value swatches of coral, terra cotta and mahogany for the flowers, and a lighter shade for the outer circle of "peacock eyes." A mottled myrtle green background was used. This piece was hooked with 1/4" strips.

Begin by hooking the central flower grouping, consisting of the flowers, leaves, and stems. Hook the flowers using simple shading techniques, hooking the four value swatch from light tips to dark centers. The leaves are hooked with lighter values at the tips, then shading darker towards the stem. This helps give dimension to the flowers and leaves.

The circle of peacock eyes are hooked next, using three rows of dip dyed, 20" strips on the outside. Start at the dark end of the strip and work towards the light end. After the three rows of dip dye are hooked, fill in the turquoise row, a row of complementary plaid, and the gold center.

The inner background of dark green is hooked in curved lines radiating from the center of the piece towards the peacock eyes. The outer rows are hooked in a circular fashion.

This old fashioned Santa is heading home after a long day of collecting Christmas trees, greens, and holly. The finished piece makes a nice pillow, wall-hanging, or framed picture.

The red used for Santa's hat and coat are bright red wool dip dyed in medium brown dye. The sky can be either dip dyed or painted in blue over white wool. Santa's bag is a spot dye of spice brown and dark brown over natural wool. The snow is a spot dye of taupe, silver gray and khaki drab over white wool. Santa's face is a wash of mahogany dye over white.

Hook Santa's face and beard first, cutting your wool in 3/32" strips to achieve the needed detail. The rest of the piece may be hooked in 1/8" strips, as pictured. The hooking order for the remainder of the piece is: shoulder strap, white trim, sleeve, sleigh rope, coat, hat, bag, gloves, boots, sleigh runner, sleigh, tree, holly berries and stems, and holly leaves.

The inside border is outlined in hunter green and filled in with a plaid of red, green, and a bit of white and blue. Most any red plaid will do. Hook the snow in straight lines, as shown. Hook the sky starting with the darkest part of the dyed wool at the top of the picture, moving toward the horizon with the light edge of the wool. Before hooking the outside border, you can place your initials at the bottom or side using the color of your choice. The outside border is hooked in rows, mitering the corners as you hook.

KRIS KRINGLE

Kris Kringle (14" x 14-1/4"), hooked by Nancy Miller, designed by Marie Beaubien.

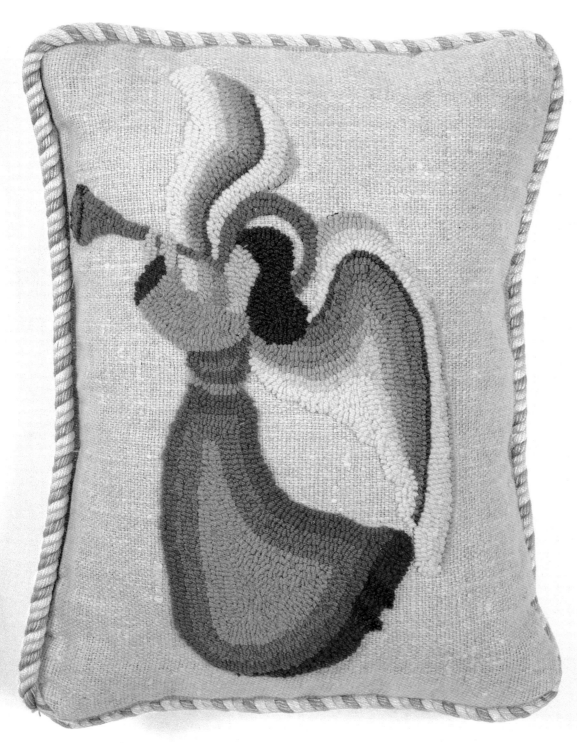

The Angel (13" x 17"), hooked by Sue Hansen from a Yankee Peddler design.

THE ANGEL

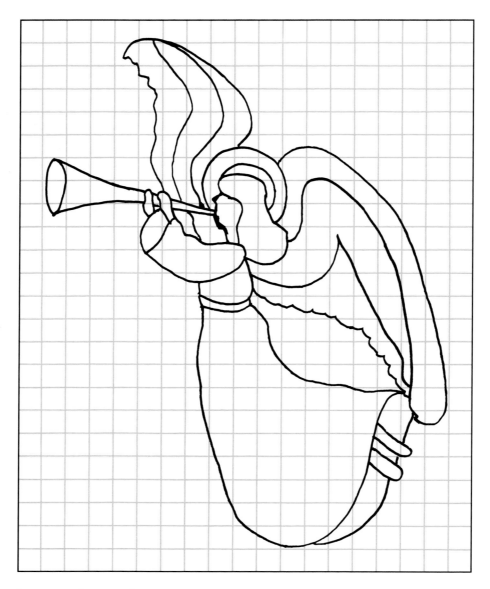

The angel motif is a popular one that recurs throughout many folk art traditions. Here we have a good example of rug hooking technique effectively adapted for use as a pillow. By using an attractive linen or monk's cloth backing, the hooked image stands out nicely by itself without a hooked background.

Although this pattern could be hooked as a primitive, 1/8" strips were used here. The color shading has been simplified into bands that occupy several rows each. These bands are created by filling in from the outer edges of the pattern, following the contours of the basic shapes.

The easiest way to obtain the colors for patterns of this kind is to purchase color gradated swatches commercially. This project was hooked using two such swatches (see photo on page 49), each of which contain several values of color.

Antigua (11" x 11-1/2"), hooked by Nancy
Miller, designed by Jane Flynn.

This simple geometric pattern is hooked in the style of a Guatemalan mola, using bright colors against black background. The strips have been cut 3/16" wide.

Any combination of bright colors of dyed or as is wool can be used. But in order to experiment with and learn a variety of dyeing techniques, a combination of animal, chemical, plant and acid dyes were used in this piece. They include:

body and head of the bird in orange, carefully staying within the lines of the pattern. As you reach the points on each diamond in the body, leave your hook inside the loop and turn the strip carefully in the new direction you will be hooking. This will help you achieve a "point" at each corner, and help in avoiding bumps on the bottom side of your hooking.

Outline the top and bottom of the bird wings

Color	Dye Source	Number of Values
Pink	Cochineal (cactus beetles)	2
Orange	Madder root	1
Turquoise green	Cushing dye	2
Yellow	Pro Chemical Acid Washfast #119	2

Before dyeing with natural dyestuffs, be sure that they yield a fast color on wool materials, and use the proper mordant. With cochineal you can obtain various yellows, pinks, reds, and purples, depending on the mordant. (Two excellent reference books on the use of natural dyes are: *The Dye Pot,* by Mary Frances Davidson; and, *Natural Dyes and Home Dyeing,* by Rita J. Adrosko.)

Begin by hooking the outline surrounding the center motifs with dark pink. Then hook one row of black inside this border and two rows on the outside. The motifs inside and outside this border will be hooked up to this band.

Next, hook the eye of the bird with dark pink. An end-loop-end is all that is needed. Hook the

with the darker value of turquoise green, then fill with the lighter value. Hook the legs in the dark yellow value, holding the lines straight and even.

To hook the diamonds, begin at the center with dark pink, then hook the outside in light pink. Fill in the middle row of the diamond with the dark shade of turquoise green.

Hook the flashes around the diamonds by alternating one row of light yellow with one row of black. Next, hook the border motif with dark turquoise green, taking care to hold the lines straight and even. All that is left is to fill in the rest of the background with jet black wool.

This piece may be finished as a pillow, bound as a table mat or wall hanging, or framed.

Primitive Flowers (20" x 30"), hooked and designed by Jane Olson.

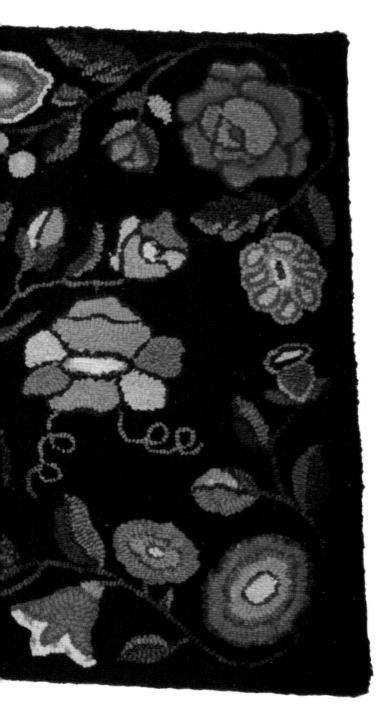

This design was inspired by antique hooked rugs. The various flower motifs were collected from numerous old patterns. It can be hooked as a sampler with almost any color combinations, and as a primitive or traditional. The strips used here were of medium width, about 3/16".

When most of the old rugs were made, hookers had very few colors to work with. Black, brown and gray were predominant because these were the practical colors used in clothing. The reds found in the early rugs were from the red flannel underwear so popular with men at that time. Other colors were dyed from roots, vegetables, bark, flowers, fruit and berries.

You will need about 2-1/2 lbs. of material to complete this pattern. This is an excellent pattern to use the woolens from your scrap bag for the flowers and leaves. You can use tweeds, plaids and checks dyed in greens, reds, blues and golds for the flower centers, outlining, stems and veins of leaves.

Background colors to use are black, navy blue, dark green, dark gray, federal blue or antique black. The dye used here was dark green over a dark blue-black check material, and the results were an antique black with a greenish cast.

There is no shading on the flowers. However, different shades of one color can be used for the various petals of the larger flowers. The flowers are repeated on both sides of the pattern. You can be creative and do each flower a different color, or repeat the same colors on both sides of the pattern. If using a dark background, outline the design in a light color or plaid material.

For this pattern, you may get better results by outlining the petals and leaves with slightly wider strips. These will hold the shape of the pattern more effectively. Follow the curves of each shape as you hook and fill.

If you are not able to gather sufficient materials from your scrap bag, another approach is spot-dyeing, dip-dyeing or jar-dyeing. You can place the fabric in a large casserole pan in several layers and pour the dye solution around the edge of the fabric. The dye works its way to the center of the fabric in wonderful patterns. When cut into strips, they can be hooked into your design with great results.

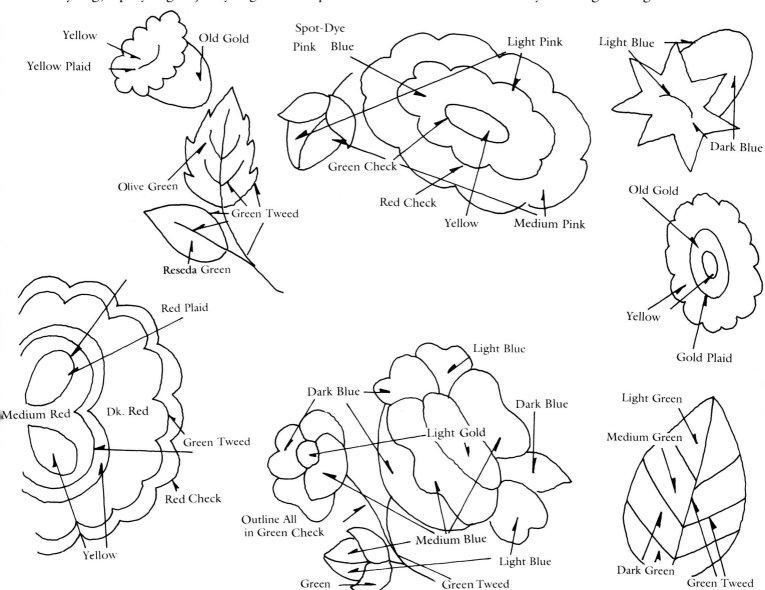

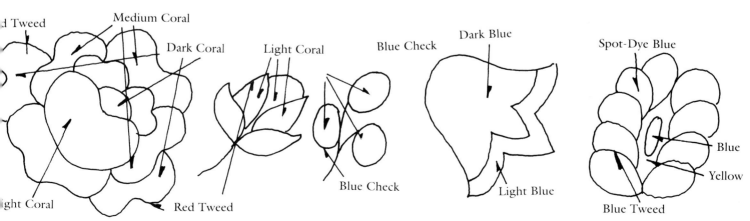

Tweed Medium Coral Dark Coral Light Coral Blue Check Dark Blue Spot-Dye Blue

Blue Check

Light Blue

Light Coral Red Tweed Blue Tweed Blue Yellow

The name of this pattern alone inspires one to think of spring colors and bright summer days. The pattern can be incorporated into any room of a home. It can be hooked as a traditional or a primitive rug, and is not too difficult for less experienced hands. The size is perfect for hooking it in a reasonable amount of time and fitting it into a small area. What better way to display this happy pattern than to use it as a wall hanging for everyone's enjoyment?

If you plan to work this pattern as a primitive, use solid colors and outline each block and each design. If working it as a traditional, use shades of swatches for the design and also outline each block.

This pattern requires 3-1/2 to 4 lbs. of material to complete the entire rug.

Hearts and Flowers (22" x 38"), hooked by **Norma Flodman, designed by Jane Olson.**

Background in Blocks (2 yds.)	**Border and Out-lining (1-1/2 yds.)**	**Hearts (1 yd. or 8 Swatches)**	**Flower Designs (3/4 yd. or 6 Swatches)**
1. Hit and Miss Colors	Black	Red or American Beauty	Turquoise
2. Pink and Violet Alternate Colors	Dark Rose-Pink	Pink	Violet
3. White	Dark Blue	Blue	Yellow

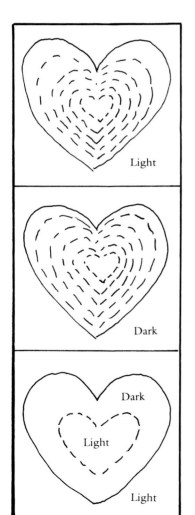

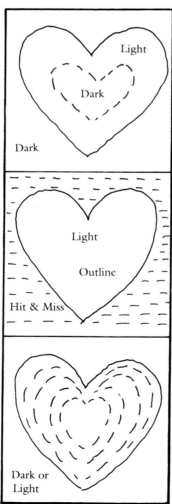

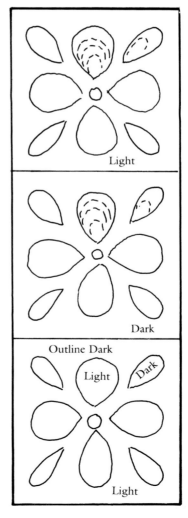

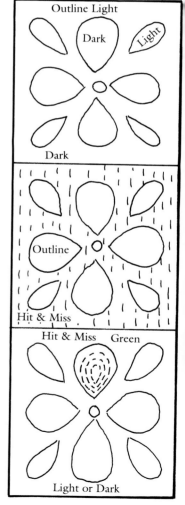

As you may see from the three suggested color schemes, there are six different ways to hook the hearts. If you are using a dark background and hooking with swatches, work the hearts from dark in the center to light on the outer edge. Reverse this process if you are using a light background. Hook in the border color for all the lines of the blocks.

Another suggestion is to use a light background in the blocks with the hearts and a dark background in the blocks containing the flower designs. This would be very effective.

If hooking this pattern as a primitive, use the same idea except outline both the hearts and the flower designs with a dark or light color depending on the color of the background. When hooking the hearts or the flower motifs, always work in the contour of the design as shown in the diagrams.

Another excellent idea for this rug, if working it as a primitive, is hooking the hearts in a multitude of colors and hooking a plain background. This can be reversed also by hooking the hearts in a solid color and the background in many colors, such as a hit and miss pattern. The same idea will work for the flower designs.

The flower designs in the diagrams are set up in the same sequence as the hearts. Here again, follow the contour of the design when hooking. If using swatches, do not try to get all the shades in the larger petals. Work the first four shades or the last four shades in the larger petals. Hook either the first two shades or the last two shades for the smaller corner petals. The smaller petals can also be treated as leaves and worked in green.

Start the petals at the point where the #1 or #6 shade is on the diagram and work to the outside. This process is the same for the hearts. By hooking the petals on any design in this way, you do not crowd the material and try to force all the shades into an area that will not accommodate it. Work only as many shades as you can. There is no rule that all six or eight shades have to fit into a certain design. Be sure not to skip a shade. There is an exception to this rule if working stems or something that has to appear rounded. You may then have to skip a shade of color.

Naomi (32" x 44"), hooked by Norma Flodman, designed by Jane Olson.

This pattern is a combination of designs from an American Indian blanket and a Navajo rug. The center motif is taken from a Chief's blanket made in the 1840s. The border, which resembles the Greek Key design, was taken from a rug pattern also made in the 1800s. The Navajo Indians were very accepting of foreign design, so it is quite possible that this border was introduced to them during this period.

The strips for this rug can be cut almost any standard width. A medium cut of 3/16" works quite nicely. You will need about 5 lbs. of material, since it is just a little under 10 square feet, and 1/2 lb. is needed for each square foot. If you are working with yardage, wool flannel by the yard weighs 3/4 of a lb., and lightweight coat wool weighs 1 lb.

A suggested amount of yardage for the center background and the background covering the area between the outside border and the key design is 3 yards. However, you may choose to use a different color for the outer background, as was done with the rug shown here.

1-3/4 yds. of material	**1 yd. of material**	**1/4 yd. of material**	**1/8 yd. of material**
Outside border. Narrow border on the key design. Wide border on the center cross design. All outlining.	Narrow border on center cross design. Wide border on key design.	Outside border on diamond design. Inside border on cross design.	Inside border of diamond design. Centers of cross designs.

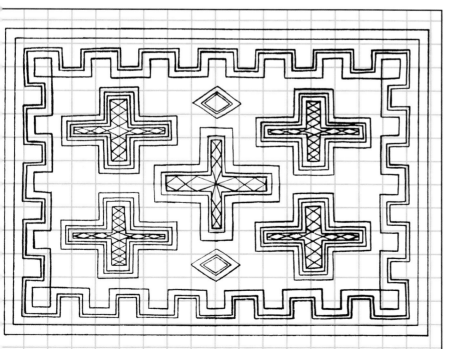

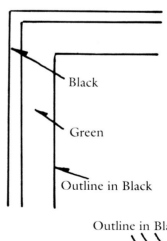

Black

Green

Outline in Black

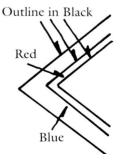

Outline in Black

Red

Blue

Color Code	A	B	C
Center Background	Natural	Taupe	Red
Background between Key Border and Outside Border	Natural	Dark Taupe	Grey-Blue
Cross Designs			
Outside Border	Green	Rust	Grey-Blue
Narrow Border	Black	Black	Navy Blue
Inside Border	Blue	Green	Dark Gray
Center Designs	Natural and Red	Natural and Rust	White and Red
Diamond Design	Red and Blue	Rust and Green	Dark Gray and Navy Blue
Key Border			
Wide Border	Green	Rust	Gray-Blue
Narrow Border	Black	Black	Navy Blue
Outside Border	Black	Black	Navy Blue

A good place to start hooking the pattern is in the center, working your way out toward the edge. By hooking in this way, you do not close yourself into an area where the threads of the rug backing become so tight that it is difficult to push the hook through the weave. This will also give a very uneven surface when hooked. Start this pattern in the center cross first, and work the background as you proceed.

If you would like to create the appearance of a woven Indian rug, hook in straight lines. This pattern is very easy to hook in this manner because of the geometric figures. Work the background in one direction. If you feel comfortable hooking from right to left, work each row in the same direction. This will give you an even surface.

When working the centers of the cross designs, hook the diagonal lines first, then fill in the centers. Hook the inside border next, and then the two outer borders of the crosses.

When you start to use the background color, outline the outer edge of each design first with the background material. This will keep the lines straight.

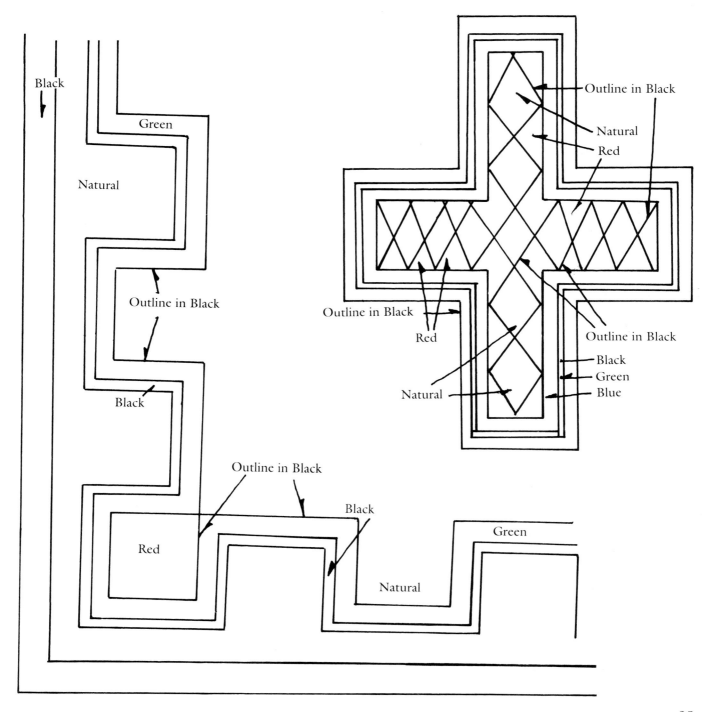

Black

Green

Natural

Outline in Black

Black

Outline in Black

Red

Outline in Black

Black

Green

Natural

Outline in Black

Natural

Red

Outline in Black

Red

Outline in Black

Black

Green

Blue

Natural

This geometric oriental is shaded one row of hooking at a time, achieving a fine gradation of hues. Strips are cut 3/32" wide.

Choosing an effective color plan is an important part of this design. Although specific colors are given here, the diagrams are keyed in such a way that you can substitute your own colors for each range. If you choose to alter the color plan, start with the background color, then the border, and so on.

The colors and amounts used in this rug are as follows:

Beige (background)	1 yd.
Rust red (borders)	3/4 yd.
Apricot	3 swatches
Juniper	2 swatches
Bronze gold	3 swatches, plus an extra piece of value #6
White	2 pieces each of values #3, 4, 5, 6

Persian Petite (22-3/4" x 35"), hooked by Meredith LeBeau from a Yankee Peddler design.

Keeping in mind that value #1 is the lightest shade and #6 is the darkest, use the following key to interpret the diagrams for color placement:

Letter on Diagram	Color Value #
Apricot	
A	1
B	2
C	3
D	4
E	5
F	6
Juniper	
G	1
H	2
J	3
K	4
L	5
M	6
Bronze Gold	
N	1
P	2
Q	3
R	4
S	5
T	6
White	
U	3
V	4
W	5
X	6

Hook the design in the center first. One row of background should be hooked around the design to keep the loops in place. Since many of the shapes in this design are delicate and narrow, be careful to stay inside the lines as you hook. Otherwise, you may not be able to crowd certain background colors into the space that remains. The large background areas should be hooked in wavy lines—not straight across.

To prevent the corners of traditionally hooked rugs from bulking up, draw a 45 degree diagonal line to miter each corner of the pattern. Rather than hooking around the corners with the same strip, stop at this line, cut the strip, then start again on the next edge.

Diagram 1

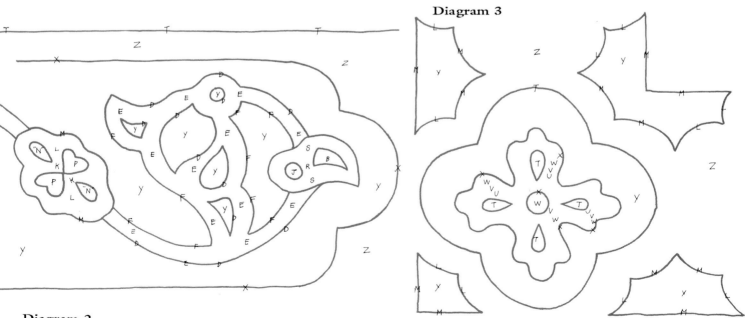

Diagram 3

Diagram 2

This is one of Pearl McGown's early patterns, adapted from a very old needlepoint design. All the strips are cut 1/8" wide. At first glance this project appears complex. Other than the brown fretwork, there are only two types of flowers and two styles of leaves, making the hooking of this rug fairly easy once the initial colors and shading are planned. The flowers are roses and padulas. Padulas are actually a make-believe flower which can be developed in any colors you wish.

Agatha Antique (30-1/2" x 60"), hooked by
Nancy Miller, designed by Pearl McGown.

The color plan for this rug may be outlined as follows:

Roses and buds: tinted shades of coral, terra cotta and mahogany
Padulas: silver gray, either dip-dyed or swatches of eight values
Flower centers: gold
Leaves: values of green and dark plaid
Rosebud tendril tips: chartreuse
Fretwork: eight values of spice brown
Backgrounds: four values of drab green
Border line: overdyed plaid

Begin by hooking the two center roses with shades of pink and the gold centers. Hook the petal closest to you first. Shade one petal at a time, moving from the front of the flower toward the back, until the flower is completed. Surround the rose with one row of background and check that there is enough contrast in value to make the rose stand out. If this is your first rose, you might trace the rose onto paper and practice shading with a pencil (or colored pencils) to determine the light and dark shadings.

Next, hook the two center padulas with an eight value swatch, dip dye, or combination of both. For the padula centers, hook a crescent of pink and fill the rest of the center with gold.

Fill in the veins of the surrounding wreath of leaves with pink. Hook the leaves using the pink end of the dyed strip for the tips, moving down the leaf as it transitions to green. Use the darkest of your strips for the leaf in the back portion of the trio. The darkest leaves and tendrils that appear in the center and corners were hooked with strips from a dark plaid shirt.

Hook the rosebuds from light at the base of the bud to dark at the tip. This will give the contrast necessary against the light background. The tips of the rose tendrils have an end, loop and end of chartreuse to emphasize the pointed tips.

Once the center floral grouping is complete, hook the fretwork. In the piece shown, the fret-

work was hooked with an imaginary light source coming from one corner of the rug. This adds dimension to the fretwork, giving the appearance of light and shadow on the imaginary carved wood. After the fretwork, hook the center background with a very pale green.

Repeat the same hooking methods on the corner floral arrangements, using a light shade of green for background. The inside border line is a terra cotta shade, then a band of light green. Next, a border line of red and navy plaid overdyed with terra cotta, and finish with a band of dark green.

103

Some twenty native species of wild rose can be found across North America. Some of these include meadow rose, prairie rose, swamp rose, and pasture rose. Perhaps you'll want to incorporate a variety that grows near you into this design.

In addition to wild roses, this soft, delicate pattern includes blue bells and wild daisies straight from the meadow. A finer cut strip will enable you to achieve the subtle shading in this traditional rug. The only real variables in the color plan are the choice of background and border scrolls.

Susan's Meadow (32" x 50" oval), hooked and designed by Jane Olson.

You will need about 5 lbs. of material to hook this rug, altogether.

Center background	1-3/4 yds. of wool (White, Natural, Celery, or any pastel shades of your choice. If you prefer a dark color, you can use Dark Green or Black.)
Border background	1-1/4 yds. of material (Use any one of the colors above or make the center light and the border dark.)
Wild roses	4 swatches (light pink)
Daisies	1 swatch (white to soft green
Blue bells	1 swatch (soft blue gray)
Rose leaves	4 swatches (soft olive green)
Daisy leaves	1 swatch (reseda green)
Blue bell leaves	1 swatch (soft gray-bronze green)
Scrolls	1/2 yd. dip-dyed material

These formulas can be used to dye white wool for the center and border backgrounds:

1/32 tsp. of black dye for the center field background (1-3/4 yds.). This is a surprise. The shade is a soft, pale off-white green-blue.

1 tsp. of black dye for the border background (1-1/4 yds.). This is a much deeper green-blue.

To dip-dye material for the scrolls, cut the 1/2 yd. of white wool into strips 18" long and 3" - 4" wide. Dissolve the following dyes in three separate containers of hot water:

(1) 1/32 tsp. - wild rose
(2) 1/8 tsp. - silver gray, 1/16 - tsp. blue
(3) 1 tsp. - olive green

Dip all the material in the wild rose solution first.

Dip 3/4 of the length of each strip in the blue solution next. Then dip 1/2 the length of each strip (the blue end) in the green solution. Because the material is now a blue color from the blue dye, the olive green dyed area will be more of a reseda green.

Start hooking the wild roses first. The petals are numbered in the diagram so that they can be hooked in that order. As you can see by the design, the petals are shaded from light in the center to dark on the outer edge. The turnovers of the petals are very light. Be sure to hook the number one shade (the lightest) around the turnover first to hold the line. The center of the flower is a green-gold color. The stamens are green tipped in the green-gold color also.

The rose to the left has not quite opened yet, but the sepals have already fallen away from the flower. Do the sepals in green of the swatch being used for the leaves of the roses. Hook the petals as numbered. When hooking the buds, do the sepals first. Then hook the petals of the bud next.

The blue bells have been added to this pattern for color. The soft blue-gray blends nicely with the muted colors of the roses and the daisies. Start with the highlight on the outside of the cup of the bell, and work to the outer edge. Outline the back side of the opening with the darker #6 shade. Fill in with the lighter shades. The pistil is gold. You can use the same gold color as you did for the center of the roses. Hook the stems with the #6 and #4 of the green swatch. If you hook only one line, this will be lost when filling in the background. The leaves are very simple. They are hooked as shown in the diagram.

The daisies call for a swatch that is gradated white to soft green. However, several other swatches can be used with the other colors in this pattern, such as white to bronze green, pale yellow to yel-

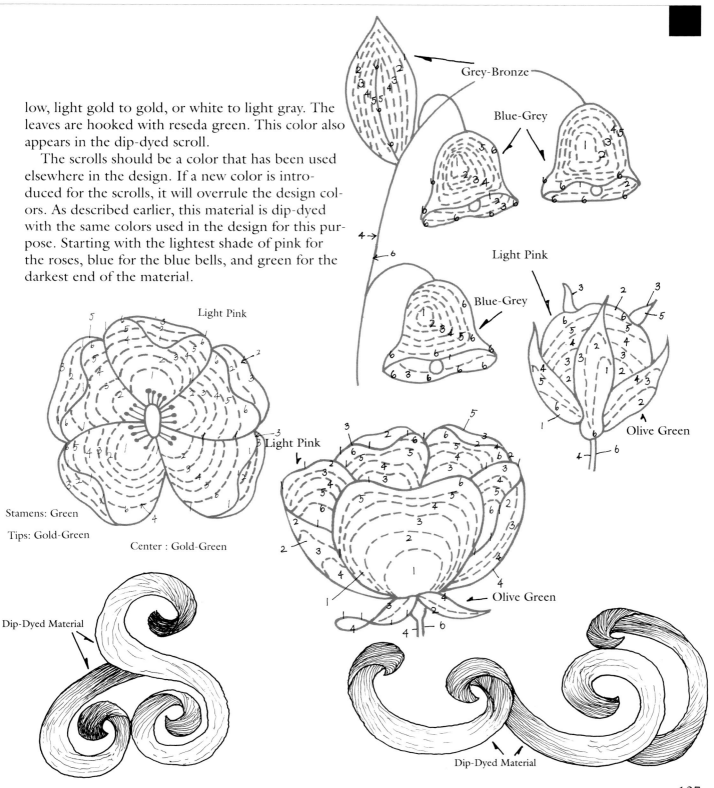

low, light gold to gold, or white to light gray. The leaves are hooked with reseda green. This color also appears in the dip-dyed scroll.

The scrolls should be a color that has been used elsewhere in the design. If a new color is introduced for the scrolls, it will overrule the design colors. As described earlier, this material is dip-dyed with the same colors used in the design for this purpose. Starting with the lightest shade of pink for the roses, blue for the blue bells, and green for the darkest end of the material!

Grey-Bronze

Blue-Grey

Light Pink

Blue-Grey

Olive Green

Light Pink

Stamens: Green

Tips: Gold-Green

Center : Gold-Green

Light Pink

Olive Green

Dip-Dyed Material

Dip-Dyed Material

Scrolls can be found everywhere. Variations of this design go back in time for thousands of years. The classical civilizations used scrolls on buildings, tiles, doorways, statues, clothing, chariots, and all kinds of art work. It is no wonder that they found their way to rug design.

Even though this pattern calls for fine shading, it can be hooked with almost any standard width of strip. Since this rug covers an area of 9-1/3 square feet, you will need between 4-1/2 and 5 lbs. of material, depending on how high you hook the loops.

Center background	2-1/2 yds. of material
Border background	1-1/2 yds. of material
Scrolls	1 yd. of dip-dyed material or 8 swatches
Flowers	5 swatches
Leaves	1/4 yd. of dip-dyed material or 2 swatches

Start with the flower in the center of the pattern. (See Diagram #1.) The centers of the flowers are very large. If a new color is introduced for the centers that is not in the rest of the color scheme, the centers will stand out like bull's eyes. Either use the green for the centers, or outline in green and fill in with the scroll color. The petals of the flowers can be worked from light in the center to dark on the outside, if using a light background. Reverse this process if using a dark background.

The flowers and buds in this rug were hooked in woodrose pinks. The leaf material can be dip-dyed by dipping light gray blue partially into a 1/2 tsp. solution of bronze green. If using a pre-dyed swatch for the leaves, see Diagram #1 for shading. The veins in the leaves can be hooked with values #4 and #6 of woodrose. Next, hook the scrolls adjacent to the flower.

Victoria Scroll
(32" x 42"),
hooked by
Norma
Flodman,
designed by
Jane Olson.

Color Options:

	A	B	C	D
Center background	Light Federal Blue	Light Beige	Black	Celery
Border background	Dark Federal Blue	Medium Brown	Black	Dark Green
Scrolls	Woodrose, Khaki Drab and Garnet	Nugget Gold, Salmon and Seal Brown	Apricot, Woodrose, and Mahogany	Old Gold, Old Rose and Olive Green
Flowers	Woodrose	Rust to Green	Apricot	Mahogany and Terra Cotta
Leaves	Bronze Green over Blue	Bronze Green over Gold	Bronze Green over Apricot	Bronze Green over Blue

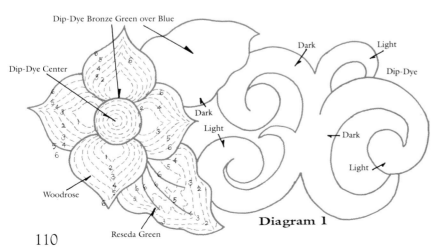

Dip-Dye Bronze Green over Blue

Dip-Dye Center

Dark

Light

Dip-Dye

Dark

Light

Dark

Light

Woodrose

Reseda Green

Diagram 1

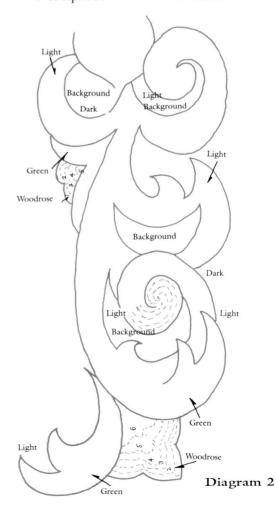

Light

Background

Light

Dark

Light
Background

Light

Green

Woodrose

Background

Dark

Light

Background

Light

Green

Woodrose

Light

Green

Diagram 2

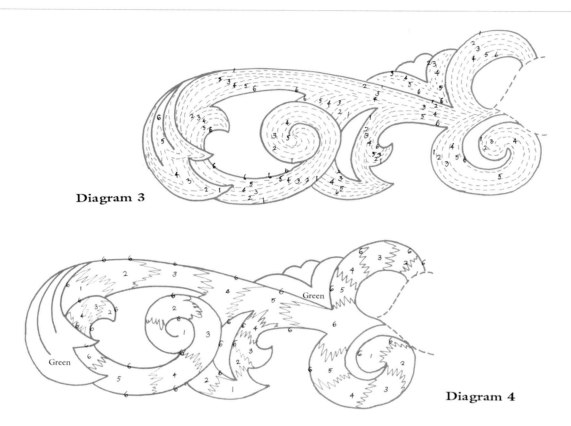

Diagram 3

Green

Green

Diagram 4

To dip-dye scroll material, first tear white wool into 18" long strips, 3" - 4" wide. Dip it all in woodrose, then 2/3 the length of the strips in khaki drab, then the bottom 1/3 in garnet. If the garnet isn't quite dark enough, add a little bronze green.

Work the background in and around the center design before starting the border scrolls and flowers. The background material can be dyed as follows:

2-1/2 yds. center
3/4 tsp. Silver Gray
1/4 tsp. Blue

1-1/2 yds. border
2-1/4 tsp. Silver Gray
3/4 tsp. Blue

This formula can be varied one way or another depending on your preference for silver gray or blue.

Start in the corners first with the turnover leaves.

(See Diagram #2.) Hook the light shade at the tips of the leaves and dark at the base. The buds in the corner are worked from dark to light, because of the dark background.

Now hook the large scrolls. Start them at the turnover leaves and work to the center on the side. There are 8 more buds and small leaves coming out of the scrolls beside the corner buds. Sometimes you cannot use all of the strip, so cut it off and put it to one side. It can be used to fill in the dark areas or light areas when needed. Fill in the background around the scrolls as you work. Be careful to fill in even the narrower areas.

Apply the same principles as you work your way around the border. If you choose to hook with swatches instead of dip-dyeing, you can follow either Diagram #3 or #4. The scroll in #4 should be outlined in a dark shade.

111

Fleur de Charme
(32" x 42"),
hooked and
designed by Jane
Olson.

This delicate floral design was inspired by an old embroidered vest. The flowers are generic and can be treated in many ways. The flowers and leaves in the center of the pattern can be life-size or bigger, while those in the border are miniaturized.

The material required for this traditional rug is 4-1/2 to 5 lbs. The strips in this rug were cut 1/8" wide.

Background	2-1/2 yds. of material
Key and Small Borders	1 yd. of material
Leaves	5 swatches Reseda Green
Star Flowers	4–5 swatches Gray-Blue or Blue
Petal Flowers	4 swatches Terra Cotta and Wine
Single Petal Flowers	4 swatches Old Gold or Gold

Suggested background colors are beige, light gray, celery green or pale blue-green. The light color background should be equivalent to the #2 shade of a swatch. If you are dyeing the 2-1/2 yds. of white background material, use 1/8 tsp. of blue and a little less than 1/32 tsp. of bright green. The amount used for the Key and Border designs is 1/4 tsp. of blue and 1/16 tsp. bright green for the 1 yd. piece.

Each of the flowers in this pattern appears in clusters of three. In the star flowers, all six shades are used, but only four at a time in any given flower. (See Diagram #1.) The centers are outlined in green and filled in with gold.

The single petal flowers are hooked entirely in shades of gold. (See Diagram #2.) The centers and petal shadings can be alternated within each cluster.

If you have chosen to use a dark background, keep in mind that all the shading sequences should be reversed.

An array of color swatches can be considered for the petal flowers. (See Diagram #3.) Pinks, violets, red grapes, plums, or purples can be used effectively. Outline the centers with a dark shade and fill in with light. Up to five shades should fit into each petal.

The leaves are very small on this pattern, particularly on the border. You may find the leaves a little tedious to hook, but the results are lovely. The stems and veins are hooked with #5 and #6 shades. The reason for using both is that you will run out

of #6 shade if using just that shade. Use both of these shades at random, except in the large curled leaf at the end of each cluster where #6 is always used. Some of the leaves in the center are a little larger than others. On these larger leaves use 6 shades; 3 on one side and 3 on the other side. This is shown in the diagram. For the smaller leaves in the center and on the border use 2 shades on one side and 2 on the other. Alternate all the shades equally throughout the leaves to prevent using too much of one shade.

The key border is hooked with one line of the dark color. Be consistent in how many rows of background are hooked in between the keys. This will keep the design geometric. Hook at least 2 straight rows above and below the keys. This will also keep them straight. The small borders (1/4")

Diagram 1

Diagram 2

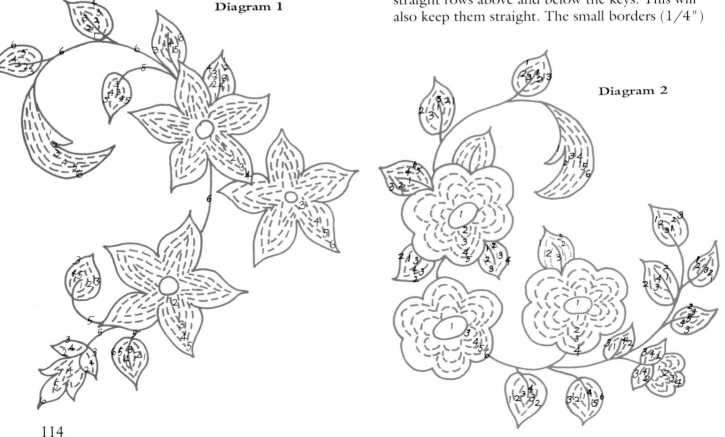

114

and the larger border (1/2") are hooked with the dark color also. Another suggestion for the 1/2" border is to outline in the dark color and fill in with either the same green as the leaves or one of the flower colors. There is a wide area between the center and the outside flower border to be worked with background. Try hooking this in straight lines and miter the corners. (See Diagram #4.)

Actually, there are many colors for flowers, leaves and background that can be used for this pattern to fit your decor. Try them.

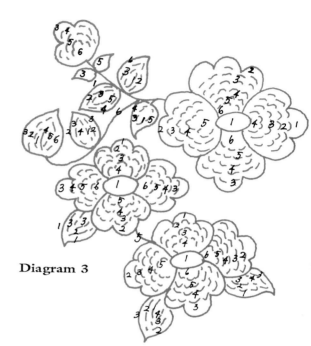

Diagram 3

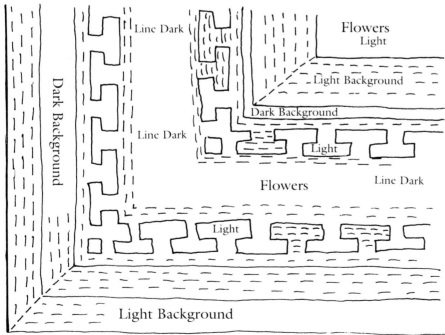

Diagram 4

These patterns have been adapted from *W.W. Kent's book* The Hooked Rug, *Pearl McGown's* The Lore and Lure of Hooked Rugs, *and Joel and Kate Kopp's* American Hooked & Sewn Rugs.

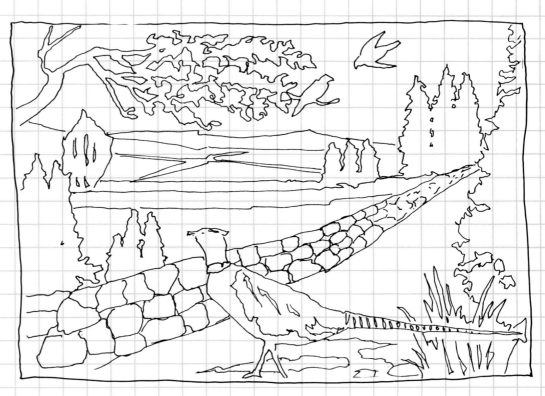

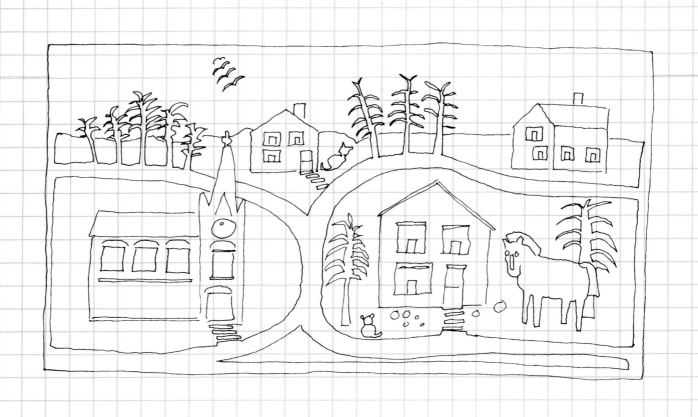

A GALLANT SHIP PUTS OUT TO SEA
ALAS MY HEART GOES WITH IT

DON'T TREAD ON ME

PLUCK MY HEART STRING CUPID
WITH ABANDON AS OF YORE

AND SEND A MAN LIKE THIS ONE
TO A LONELY WIDOWS DOOR

HERE HOOKED IS A PICTURE OF MY HUSBANDS KIN ILL BE GLAD WHEN I DIE AND DON'T SEE THEM AGAIN

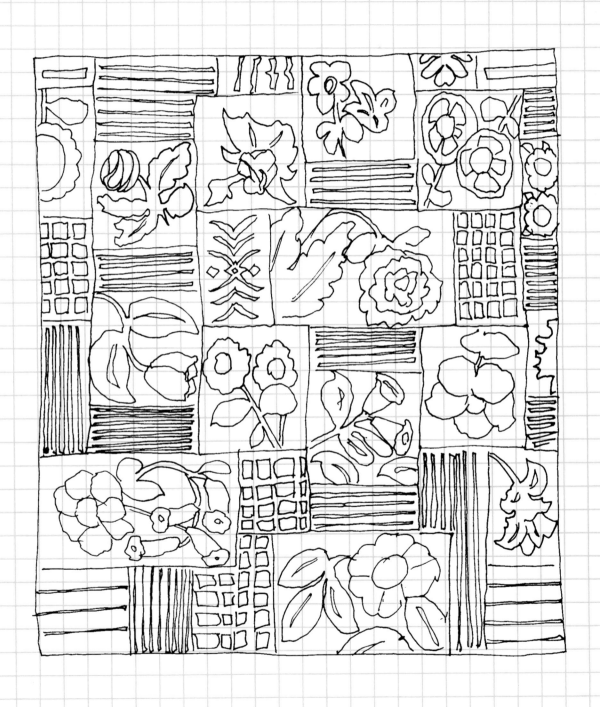

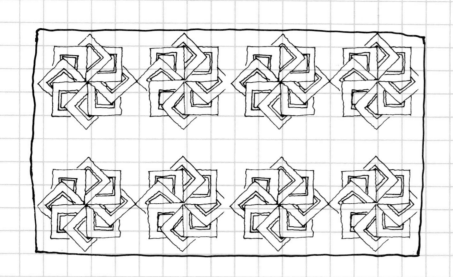

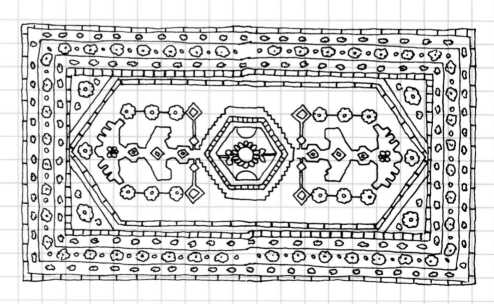

134

DIRECTORY OF RUG HOOKING ARTISTS

■

Anne Ashworth & Jean
Armstrong
Green Mountain Rug School
RD 1, Box 358
Randolph Center, VT 05061

Marie Azzaro
Yankee Peddler Hooked Rugs
57 Saxonwood Rd.
Fairfield, CT 06430
**(Patterns, Supplies, Rug
Dealer)**

D. Marie Bresch
4051 Levi Gulch
Carson City, NV 89703
**(Design, Instruction,
Restoration)**

Mary Sheppard Burton
21,600 Davis Mill Rd.
Germantown, MD 20876
**(Instruction, Commissioned
Work)**

Sally Corbett
2085 Oakmont Way
Eugene, OR 97401

Gloria E. Crouse
4325 John Luhr Road, NE
Olympia, WA 98506
(206) 491-1980
**(Instruction, Supplies,
Commissioned Work)**

Nancy Greenberg
25 Spring Cove Court
Arden, NC 28704
(Instruction, Supplies)

Marion N. Ham
Quail Hill Designs
4018 Pennellville Rd.
Brunswick, ME 04011
**(Instruction, Patterns,
Supplies)**

Jacqueline L. Hansen
237 Pine Point Rd.
Scarborough, ME 04074
(Instruction, Patterns, Kits)

Virginia Hildebrant
Ginny's Gems
5167 Robinhood Drive
Willoughby, OH 44094
(Patterns, Supplies)

Peg Irish
114 Metoxit Road
Waquoit, MA 02536

Meredith P. LeBeau
The Elbeau Room
9 Elm Avenue
Salem, MA 01970
(Instruction, Supplies)

Maryanne Lincoln
139 Park Street
Wrentham, MA 02093
(Instruction)

Roslyn Logsdon
Weaver's Loft, M.C.A.C.
12826 Laurel-Bowie Rd.
Laurel, MD 20708
(Custom Patterns)

Chris Merryman
26449 Circle Drive, NW
Poulsbo, WA 98370
(Commissioned Work)

Nancy Miller
2251 Ralston Road
Sacramento, CA 95821
(Instruction, Supplies, Kits)

Kathy Morton
Morton House Primitives
9860 Crestwood Terrace
Eden Prairie, MN 55347
(Instruction, Patterns)

Joan Moshimer
Rug Hooker Studio
Box 351, North St.
Kennebunkport, ME 04046
**(Instruction, Patterns,
Supplies)**

Jane Olson
Rug Studio
P.O. Box 351
Hawthorne, CA 90250
also: 5400 W. 119th St.
Inglewood, CA 90304
**(Instruction, Patterns,
Supplies)**

Beth Sekerka
Hooked on Rugs
44492 Midway Drive
Novi, MI 48375
(Patterns, Kits)

Lorna Smith
1130 Colby Avenue
Everett, WA 98201

Ann Winterling
61 Mountain Road
Concord, NH 03801
(Instruction, Custom Design)

ACKNOWLEDGEMENTS

We wish to thank the following suppliers:

W. Cushing & Company
Box 351, North Street
Kennebunkport, ME 04046
(207) 967-3711
(Dyes, Supplies)

Davidson's Old Mill Yarn
P.O. Box 8
Eaton Rapids, MI 48827
(517) 663-2711
(Wool yarns, Mill ends)

The Dorr Mill Store
P.O. Box 88
Guild, NH 03754
(603) 863-1197
(Wool yardage, Supplies)

Forestheart Studio
21 South Carroll St.
Frederick, MD 21701
(301) 695-4815
(Supplies)

Harry M. Fraser Co.
R. & R. Machine Co., Inc.
Rt. 3, Box 254
Stoneville, NC 27048
(919) 573-9830
(Cutters, Supplies)

Jane McGown Flynn, Inc.
P.O. Box 301
Sterling Junction, MA 01565
(508) 365-7278
(Supplies, Designs)

PRO Chemical & Dye, Inc.
P.O. Box 14
Somerset, MA 02726
(508) 676-3838
(Dyes, Supplies)

Rittermere-Hurst-Field
45 Tyler St., Box 487
Aurora, Ontario L4G 3L6
CANADA (416) 841-1616
(Supplies)

A complete listing of suppliers may be obtained from: Rug Hooking Magazine, P.O. Box 15760, Cameron & Kelker Streets, Harrisburg, PA 17105
1-800-233-9015, ext. 50

SUGGESTED READING

Ashworth, Anne & Jean Armstrong. *Green Mountain Colors.* Randolph Center, VT: Green Mountain Rug School, 1985.

Batchelder, Martha. *The Art of Hooked-Rug Making.* Camden, ME: Down East Books, 1947.

Beatty, Alice & Mary Sargent. *Basic Rug Hooking.* Harrisburg, PA: Stackpole Books, 1990.

Blumenthal, Betsy & Kathryn Kreider. *Hands on Dyeing.* Loveland, CO: Interweave Press, 1988.

_____ . *A Celebration of Hand-Hooked Rugs.* Ed., Staff of *Rug Hooking* Magazine. Harrisburg, PA: Stackpole Books, 1991.

Crouse, Gloria E. *Hooking Rugs: New materials, new techniques* (and companion video).

Newtown, CT: The Taunton Press, 1990.

DiFranza, Happy & Steve. *Hooking Fine Gifts.* Harrisburg, PA: Stackpole Books, 1992.

Field, Jeanne. *Shading Flowers.* Harrisburg, PA: Stackpole Books, 1991.

Hornafius, Pat. *Country Rugs.* Harrisburg, PA: Stackpole Books, 1992.

Kent, W.W. *The Hooked Rug.* Reprint of 1941 ed. Detroit: Gale Research, 1971.

Kopp, Joel & Kate Kopp. *American Hooked and Sewn Rugs.* New York: E.P. Dutton & Co., 1975.

McGown, Pearl K.. *Color in Hooked Rugs,* Boston: Buck Printing Co., 1954.

McGown, Pearl K.. *The Lore and*

Lure of Hooked Rugs. Acton, MA: Acton Press, 1966.

Moshimer, Joan. *The Complete Rug Hooker.* Boston: New York Graphic Society, 1975.

Rug Hooking Magazine. P.O. Box 15760, Harrisburg, PA 17105.

Turbayne, Jessie A.. *Hooked Rugs: History & the Continuing Tradition.* Westchester, PA: Schiffer Publishing, 1991.

Wiseman, Ann. *Rug Hooking & Rag Tapestries.* New York: Van Nostrand Reinhold Co., 1969.

Zarbock, Barbara J. *The Complete Book of Rug Hooking.* New York: Van Nostrand Reinhold Co., 1961.

INDEX

METRIC EQUIVALENCY

Inches	CM
1/8	0.3
1/4	0.6
3/8	1.0
1/2	1.3
5/8	1.6
3/4	1.9
7/8	2.2
1	2.5
1-1/4	3.2
1-1/2	3.8
1-3/4	4.4
2	5.1
2-1/2	6.4
3	7.6
3-1/2	8.9
4	10.2
4-1/2	11.4
5	12.7
6	15.2
7	17.8
8	20.3
9	22.9
10	25.4
11	27.9
12	30.5
13	33.0
14	35.6
15	38.1
16	40.6
17	43.2
18	45.7
19	48.3
20	50.8
21	53.3
22	55.9
23	58.4
24	61.0
25	63.5
26	66.0
27	68.6
28	71.1
29	73.7
30	76.2
31	78.7
32	81.3
33	83.8
34	86.4
35	88.9
36	91.4